OPENING
DOORS

A SEEKER'S
REFLECTIONS ON THE ROOMS OF
CHRISTIAN LIVING

KEVIN TRESTON

Tony

Kevin

**COVENTRY
PRESS**

Published in Australia by

Coventry Press
33 Scoresby Road
Bayswater Vic. 3153
Australia

ISBN 9780648566106

Copyright © Kevin Treston 2019

Cataloguing-in-Publication entry is available from the National Library of Australia http:/catalogue.nla.gov.au/.

Cover design by Ian James - www.jgd.com.au
Design by Megan Low, FSG

Printed in Australia

CONTENTS

INTRODUCTION

Remember the first time you opened a door to a new room or new house? What happened?

In this book, I'm inviting you to open eleven doors to eleven rooms that reflect on living your Christian faith.

One of my favourite quotes in the Scriptures is, *Listen! I am standing at the door knocking; if you hear my voice and open the door, I will come in to you and eat with you and you with me* (Revelation 3:20). This verse evokes an image of a follower of Jesus, opening the door to welcome the Divine Presence for intimate conversations.

Even a casual observation of the religious landscape can see that Christianity, especially in the West, is undergoing a momentous transformation. The crisis in sexual abuse by clergy and Religious has traumatised many of the faithful whose trust in church leadership has been eroded. However, there are also encouraging signs of a stirring of the Spirit leading faith communities towards a deeper appreciation of what the Christ story means in our contemporary world. What is happening and why is this happening now? How does this transformation affect the ways people live their Christian faith? How do people live their Christian faith today?

* * * * *

One approach to exploring this transformation is to offer a profile of a series of 'doors' that open to the various 'rooms' of contemporary Christian living.

In this book, you are invited to open a series of faith doors that lead to diverse rooms of your Christian faith journey. Each room offers a perspective on contemporary reflections on living the Christian Story today. There is no attempt to summarise the theological thinking of any specific room but merely an *orientation* to some features of the Christian faith living in this room. The brevity of proposing themes in each room is more by way of suggesting a *flavour* of that aspect of the Christian life and certainly not a summary of church teachings about that theme.

I encourage you to enter each room with a heart that is open to the Spirit. I hope that you will reflect, pray, study and engage in conversations with others about how your faith life may be both challenged and deepened by your experience in these 'faith rooms'. Bring your own wisdoms and life experiences to the rooms you enter.

* * * * *

The themes in the book reflect my own personal experiences in the Christian faith and beliefs gained from over sixty years of public ministry in several countries, conversations with thousands of people seeking to live their Christian faith as well as theological studies at the doctoral and post-doctoral levels in the USA. Although my perspective is from the lens of a married person in a Western country and my religious tradition is Catholic, I suggest that many of the themes in the various rooms are relevant to all Christians in a global world.

It is assumed that multi-cultural, diverse Christian traditions will highlight themes that differ from the themes presented in the rooms. Global migration movements of peoples in our world today ensure that Christian churches generally now are very culturally diverse, not just in theology, but in how such faith communities worship and proclaim the gospel. A Christian in China, Egypt or Fiji would propose different doors and different rooms from the ones described here. Ecumenical gatherings involving people from religions other than Christian bring the richness of their traditions to a quest to be religious in rapidly changing societies.

As you open each door and reflect on that room, I encourage you to modify the reflections in that room according to your national and multicultural heritage as well as your own Christian tradition.

Personal observations on the pastoral landscape and research point to an increasing disengagement from the institutional church in the West. Each week in USA, 150 to 200 churches close their doors. Nevertheless, conversations with people also reveal a desire to follow spiritual paths and celebrate the heritage of their Christian faith although a majority perceive the church is now irrelevant in their lives. Surveys indicate that they are departing, sometimes in sorrow or indifference, sometimes in anger at a church that seems no longer to speak to them. There is a rapid rise in the numbers of 'nones' (spiritual but not affiliated with church) in Western countries.

* * * * *

In the book, I choose the term 'seekers' to describe those willing to enter the series of rooms. In his book *A Secular Age* (Cambridge, Mass. Harvard University Press, 2007) Charles Taylor, the emeritus professor at McGill University, uses the term 'dwellers' for those who are content to live out their Christian life according to fidelity as to how they understand traditional beliefs. Taylor distinguishes these from 'Seekers' who are searching to reconcile their Christian faith with new knowledge and emerging levels of religious and personal consciousness, the social sciences and cosmology. Although other commentators on the religious landscape suggest other categories of faith groups, I prefer the term 'seekers' to describe those who are open to deepen their Christian faith through discernment, study, prayer, conversations and proactive faith commitment. 'Seekers' too may be considered conservative as they return to the primal traditions of the Jesus story.

One day, perhaps well into the future, there will be a major church project to compose a new 'Summa'. The new 'Summa' will not be the work of a solitary monk like St Thomas Aquinas of medieval times, but a distillation of wisdom about the Christian story, drawn from the scholarship of theologians, cosmologists, scientists, social scientists and spiritual guides working together in partnership to compose a Credo that reframes the Christ story within the wondrous story of the universe. Or, perhaps, given the speed of evolutionary developments in science and global consciousness, there will never be another 'Summa' because any such composition will be quickly dated by dramatic evolutionary scientific advances.

> *What is increasingly clear is that the Christian church in the 21st century is on the cusp of a great evolutionary leap in consciousness through the integration of modern cosmology, science (especially quantum physics) and evolutionary consciousness with a more inclusive appreciation of what the Incarnation means. There will be a reframing of the Christian Story within this global vision of humanity, within the wondrous Universe Story. A New Story is emerging.*

The rooms offered in this book have no such pretensions of anything resembling some type of 'Summa'. The rooms are offered as simple distillations of selected contemporary Christian thinking and living through following God's revelation in Jesus as the Christ within an evolving universe. It is increasingly evident from historical studies that some accretions to church life and doctrines have obscured God's revelation in Jesus. Historical studies illuminate why certain doctrines or church laws emerged at particular epochs. However, some of these teachings have lost their relevance in today's world. The enterprise of discerning the core message of Jesus and discarding the cultural and historical accumulations of the 2000 year old Christ story is indeed a complex one involving shared conversations, studies in theology and Scripture, philosophy and history, discernment, enculturation, spirituality and global cultural consciousness.

The axis question is whether certain doctrines, canon laws and church practices enhance or diminish the gospel at this time in the Christian story. Good theology will always interpret the Christian story in language, metaphors, rituals and symbols that are attuned to contemporary consciousness as well as grounded in its core belief heritage. To what extent can there be scope for cultural diversity in how the Christian faith is taught and lived while accepting a centralised authority? How do local faith communities balance tensions between enculturation and acceptance of a corpus of teachings and worship specified by a global ecclesial authority?

* * * * *

In composing this book, I am encouraged by the urging of Pope Francis in the Apostolic Constitution *Veritatis Gaudium* (29 January 2018) where he urges the faithful to pursue a 'wise and courageous renewal' of ecclesiastical studies. His emphasis on a 'Synodal' church insists that the whole People of God are to discern a way forward for the church.

Jesus reminds us that, *In my Father's house, there are many dwelling places* (John 14:2). There are as *many dwelling places* for living the Christian faith as there are people. Everyone's spiritual path is unique to that person. When you reflect on each of the rooms, you may well ask yourself which room appeals to you now in your faith journey? How might I grow as a spiritual person using the insights from this room?

* * * * *

The book is for general readers and offered as a resource for personal and small self-directed group gatherings. It must be emphasised again that this book is not intended as some kind of summary of teachings about the Christian faith but as a resource for individuals and small groups to read, reflect and share their own insights about significant contemporary understandings of their Christian faith. I would encourage readers to jot down personal insights in a journal as well as add other themes in specific rooms.

The faith rooms are not in sequences. Individuals or groups may choose any room for their reflection and conversation according to the degree of relevance for people at that time. Why not choose the room that is most relevant for you or your group now?

A motivation for writing this book is my passion for adult life and faith formation throughout years of teaching and conferencing in several countries. All too frequently, I encounter people in parishes and faith groups who have been neglected of opportunities to nurture their adult faith life. Why adult life and faith formation is not a major goal in the evangelising mission of the church is incomprehensible to me.

* * * * *

Thanks for all those who have shared with me their faith journey stories over the years. In a sense the story told here is as much a compilation of your stories as well as my own research and faith journey.

I wish to offer thanks and appreciation to those who offered helpful comments: Garry Everett, Kay Herington, Stephen Jorgensen, Yuri Koszarycz, Ralph Arnell FMS, Janet Galos, Judy Brown, Bob Cullen, Pat Condon, Br Brian Grenier CFC, Brian Blaney, Laraine Roberts, Helen and Bernard Treston, Peter Butler, Patricia McCormack RSM, Elaine Wainright RSM.

A special thanks to Kathryn for her unfailing patience and support during the writing. Thanks also to our dog Darcy's patiently sitting beside me during long hours of writing.

In particular I wish to thank George Kendall who is always so generous in his support and advice on formatting and technical support. Thanks to Helen Treston for her proof reading. Thanks also the publishing company and in particular Hugh McGinlay and Coventry Press.

I dedicate this book to the memory of two people, Daniel O'Leary and Denis Edwards, who died while I was finalising the draft of this book (March 2019). The writings of both Daniel and Denis have been and are now an inspiration for me and all 'seekers'.

* * * * *

At the conclusion of each room there is a suggested format of:

> *Personal Responses* (your own journal jottings, icons, images, mantras, songs, Scripture references)

> *Self-directed Group Conversation Starters* (suggested questions to stimulate conversations among members of the group)

I encourage you to open the doors and let the light of the Spirit come into the rooms of your Christian Living

Kevin Treston

OPENING DOORS

But whenever you pray, go into your room and shut the door and pray to your Father who is in secret; and your Father who sees in secret will reward you.
Matthew 6:6

Creativity means to push open the heavy, groaning doorway of life itself. This is not an easy task. Indeed, it may be the most severely challenging struggle there is.
Daisaku Ikeda

Ask, and it will be given you; search and you will find; knock, and the door will be opened for you.
Matthew 7:7

The doors we open and close each day decide the lives we live.
Flora Whittemore

At the same time pray for us as well that God will open to us a door for the word, that we may declare the mystery of Christ
Colossians 4:3

There is always one moment in childhood when the door opens and lets the future in.
Graeme Green

When I came to Troas to proclaim the good news of Christ, a door was opened for me in the Lord.
2 Corinthians 2:12

When one door of happiness closes, another opens: but often we look so long at the closed door that we do not see the one which has been opened for us.
Helen Keller (1880-1968)

When they arrived, they called the church together and related all that God had done with them, and how he had opened the door of faith for the Gentiles.
Acts 14: 27

If opportunity doesn't knock, build a door.
Milton Berle

So again, Jesus said to them, 'Very truly, I tell you, I am the gate for the sheep'.
John 10:7

Teachers open a door; you enter by yourself.
Chinese proverb

The world is full of people who have never since childhood met an open doorway with an open mind.
E. B. White

But at times I think Jesus may be knocking from the inside so we will let him out.
Pope Francis's speech to Cardinals in Rome 12 March 2013.

Listen! I am standing at the door, knocking; if you hear my voice and open the door, I will come in to you and eat with you, and you with me.
Revelation 3:20

Old ways won't open new doors.
Author unknown

*A door opens in the centre of our being and we seem to fall through
it into immense depths, which – although they are infinite – are still
accessible to us.*
Thomas Merton

One may view the 2000 year old journey
of the Christian story as an unfolding of
three great movements that narrate how the
Christian story was, and is now, told, lived and
celebrated.
Each of the eleven doors in this book opens up
to eleven rooms of how this Christian Story is
experienced.

THREE GREAT MOVEMENTS IN THE 2000 YEAR OLD CHRISTIAN STORY

THE BEGINNING: God's revelation in Jesus as the Christ: Jewish heritage is the primal setting for how Jesus as the Christ story is told and celebrated.

TRADITIONAL STORY: The Christian story is shaped by Greek philosophies and Roman/European cultures from 4th century until our present age.

EMERGING COSMIC STORY: In the 21st century, there is now evolving a reframing of the Christian story (teachings, theology, spirituality, liturgy, ethical living) within the amazing story of the universe, modern science and new consciousness.

DOOR TO ROOM 1
GRACING THE EVERYDAY

Let us open the door of Room One and enter the room of gracing everyday living

How does your faith life touch your everyday happenings?

CHANGING TIMES

As a child growing up on a sugar cane farm in North Queensland, I cherish memories of my mother sitting on the end of our beds in the evening, overseeing our prayers and teaching us from the Penny Catechism. I still have this Catechism. Only once can I ever remember night prayers being abruptly terminated. Howling winds and lashing cyclonic rain drumming on the farmhouse would never interrupt this nightly ritual except... in the middle of reciting a prayer one evening, my mother suddenly said, 'Stop, and come inside from the verandah'. A large, black swamp snake was coiled on the low rafter (no ceiling) just above our heads. End of prayer.

During childhood, my Christian faith was secure in the Questions and Answers of the Penny Catechism and the ordered sequence of prayers: Our Father, Hail Mary, Prayer to Guardian Angels, Act of Contrition, Hail Holy Queen. The nightly prayers and Penny Catechism reflected a safe and unchanging religious faith. The doctrines of the church were unambiguous. To get to heaven was to follow faithfully what the church taught.

Today, it would not be a deadly, black swamp snake that stopped night prayers but, in the unlikely event of family night prayers being proposed, it would be the challenge of trying to get the children to switch off their computer games from their iPads that would make the daunting prospect of family prayers even more remote.

Just consider the following extract from the *Catholic Encyclopedia* (1914), a statement that would have been the official church position in my childhood years on the status of clergy in relationship to laity and a dominant assertion in church teachings for hundreds of years:

> '*The church is a perfect society, though all therein are not equal; it is composed of two kinds of members: in the first place, those who are depositaries of sacred or spiritual authority under its triple aspect, government, teaching and worship i.e. the clergy, the sacred hierarchy established by divine law; in the second place, those over whom this power is exercised, those who are governed, taught and sanctified, the Christian people, the laity... But the laity are not the depositaries of spiritual power; they are the flock confided to the care of the shepherds who are instructed in the word of God, the subjects who are guided by the successors of the Apostles towards the last end, which is eternal life, such is the constitution which our Saviour has given to his church*'.

Note, 'the laity are *not* (my italics) the depositaries of spiritual power'.

How times have changed or have they really?

It is mind boggling to consider how a mere eighty years later since my childhood years until the present time, so much has been upended, not just in society, technology and cultural consciousness but in how the Christian faith is lived and proclaimed. Church teachings based on 'rule by fear' have long lost any motivation for Christian living.

Many of the previous religious securities in the Christian faith of my childhood days have dissipated and new religious horizons have dawned. For example, the amazing insights emanating from cosmology and evolution challenge Christians to situate God's revelation in Jesus as the Christ firmly within a cosmic context.

There are new understandings of sexuality arising from studies in genetics. The internet has revolutionised the way people communicate. For the first time in history, every single person in the whole world who has internet access can send and receive global information. Never before has such an extraordinary phenomenon happened. Quantum physics teaches us that we live in a relational world of connected energies. Almost seventy million people are wandering the globe as refugees. In 2018, there were six hundred million people living in extreme poverty. Rampant materialism is suffocating religion in Western societies.

For over a thousand years, the church taught that outside the church there is no salvation (see *Unam Sanctam* of Pope Boniface VIII in 1302 and *Cantate Domino* of Pope Eugene IV in 1441). The Second Vatican Council (1962-1965) discarded teachings of exclusion and taught how God's presence resides in a pluralism of religions. Such teachings proclaimed by the Council will never be reversed.

DECLINE IN RELIGIOUS AFFILIATION IN WESTERN COUNTRIES

A monumental challenge for Western Christianity today is the growing number of people – especially young people – who profess little interest in organised religion. Surveys of most Western generation Z people (born between mid 1990s to early 2000s) indicate that 52% do not identify with any religion (Australian Generation Z

Study 2017). The AGZ Study was conducted by researchers from the universities of Monash, ANU and Deakin (Australia).

A younger generation tends to look to the greater certainty of science to give them answers to life questions rather than religion. For a younger generation, life experiences have a greater veracity than what authority figures tell them to believe. Young people can tend to distrust adults who have let them inherit a world with major ecological disasters in the making.

One interesting finding of the AGZ study was that this generation indicates that they were often interested in ways of being spiritual but not religious. They would be much more inclined, for example, to assist refugees to learn English than go to church. There is also a growing atheism among a younger generation who simply reject out of hand any notion of God or religious belief.

Apart from a minority of Christians who regularly attend liturgical services and programs such as National Evangelisation Team Ministries (NET) and ALPHA, many people still encounter some expressions of church life from time to time through such events as attending a church wedding or funeral, childrens sacrament programs, charitable services such as St Vincent de Paul and Salvation Army, participation with their children in faith based schools, Christmas carol singing, Bible groups, chaplains, joining causes for justice and environment or watching media programs that focus on religious questions. However, for the great majority of people, especially the younger generation in Western countries, the church seems to exist on another planet.

For those who are engaged in the evangelising mission of the church, there is a prospect of seeking common ground with those who face the daily questions of their lives. Tantalising questions that surface in our consciousness might be, 'Does the Christ story have anything to say to me about such life challenges as, studying, looking for a job, involvement in family life, financial stress, loneliness or social isolation, chronic illness, death, what is the future for my kids? If not, why then should I even bother about religion?'

Guiding questions for a person of religious faith might be:

How might I be more kind and gracious in this world?

Where and how do I find motivation to be a spiritual person?

SPIRITUALITY FOR NOW

One of the most obvious examples of contemporary spirituality and theology is the current emphasis on 'here-and-now' spirituality rather than 'after-death' spirituality. 'After-death' spirituality placed great emphasis on following the laws of the church or the Bible to ensure 'getting to heaven' and avoiding hell. For much of Christian history, the brief time on earth was considered to be little more than a testing time for the prospect of eternal life. A verse from the influential evangelical preacher John Wesley (1703-1791) sums up the 'after-death' theology:

Strangers and pilgrims here below.
The earth we know is not our place;
And hasten through this vale of woe;
And restless to behold your face.

The word 'salvation'(*sozo:* Greek for 'healing') became to be generally understood in Christian beliefs as securing eternal life with God rather than the original meaning of being reconciled and healed (see Luke 19:9).

Any exploration into contemporary theology and spirituality would surely begin, not with a summary of Christian doctrines or the Bible, but with daily experiences of how faith might be evident and relevant in our lives. Such life experiences as parenting, financial worries, the wellbeing of our children, issues of justice in our communities, health concerns, incidence of mental health, refugees, fragility of the environment, homelessness, absorb our energies and are the real agenda of our spirituality. If Christians take seriously the Incarnation, *And the Word became flesh and lived among us* (John 1:14), then grace awaits them wherever they are and however they feel.

According to the First Epistle of John, *We declare to you what was from the beginning, what we have heard, what we have seen with our eyes, what we have looked at and touched with our hands, concerning the word of life* (1 John 1:1).

When Christian living no longer encounters grace within the comings and goings of life, then the Christian faith is little more than convenient spiritual escapism. Theology that is detached from any relevance to God in the ebb and flow of daily happenings is a flight into a bubble of pious intellectualism. It is surprising and even scandalous to hear some Christian evangelists and conservative Christians mock the concept of 'the common good' and denounce social justice teachings as 'communism'. In such a worldview of bloated capitalism, becoming wealthy is proclaimed as a sign of God's blessings while being poor is an indication of God's disapproval.

THE MALAISE OF DUALISM

One of the most pernicious features in the history of Christian spirituality has been dualism, the split between body and spirit, with an assumption that life on earth was a testing ground to see if we are worthy of heaven. The roots of this dualism have complex origins in philosophies emanating from Gnosticism (Jesus was wholly divine, his humanity was an illusion), spirit versus body philosophies, Plato's alienation from the body and how monasticism seemed to offer a more certain way of securing salvation through renunciation of 'the world' (see O'Loughlin, F. *This Time of the Church*, 57).

John's Gospel has verses such as, *If the world hates you, be aware that it hated me before it hated you. If you belonged to the world, the world would love you as its own. Because you do not belong to the world, but I have chosen you out of the world – therefore the world hates you* (15:18-19). A literal reading of the text seems to reinforce a dualism between spirit and body, heaven and 'world'. When Pope Francis, on a papal visit to UAE in February 2019, called out to the crowd, 'Who is correct here, Jesus or the world?', we know that he was alluding to the clash between the gospel and values of materialism. However, implying any dichotomy between 'Jesus' and 'world' reinforces the dualism of body/spirit, world, heaven.

The oft used term 'world' in Christian spirituality is an inadequate translation of a concept meaning ideologies of consumerism and individualism. Such a designation of 'world' flatly contradicts the essential belief in the incarnation (John 1:14). After all, don't Christians believe that *God so loved the world that he gave his only son* (John 3:16)?

Where do you see the challenges of dualism in how people live their Christian faith today?

CHURCH IN WORLD

The church's long tradition of upholding beliefs that the church was a 'Perfect Society' as stated in the *Catholic Encyclopedia* of 1914 assumed that the church had nothing to learn from 'the world'. As a 'perfect society', the church, especially during the nineteenth century, generally resisted and stood apart from the dynamic, political and scientific revolutions happening after the Enlightenment (see *Syllabus of Errors* Pope Pius IX 1864). During the early twentieth century, the church became more and more marginalised from mainstream cultural and scientific movements.

One response to the dramatic decline of the church in the late 20th century in the West was a return to a nostalgic populism and fundamentalism. Christian fundamentalism, especially in the Baptist and Presbyterian Churches in USA, grew rapidly in the late 19th and early 20th centuries as a reaction to modern thinking. Fundamentalism espoused a conviction that a return to venerable faith certainties would purportedly lead estranged Christians back to the faith.

We know that there is no going back to a world gone by. We cannot live with an illusion that the internet and globalisation do not exist. As resurrection people, the future is always beckoning the pilgrim faith community courageously forward in hope.

The Second Vatican Council (1962-1965) insisted that the trials and tribulations of the world were the trials and tribulation of the mission of the church. The Pastoral Constitution of the Church in the Modern World *Gaudium et Spes* (7 December 1965) stated, *The joys and hopes, the griefs and the anxieties of the men of this age, especially those who are poor or in any way afflicted, these are the joys and hopes, the griefs and anxieties of the followers of Christ.*

As we open the door and enter the first room, we are encouraged by a belief in how the oneness of our being with God is woven into the dynamics of everyday happenings. Such a realisation is not a separation of spirit from body, not a division between world and heaven but right there in the FAITH AWARENESS of every moment of our days. For a person of faith, a sense of transcendence may be experienced in surfing, gardening, walking your dog, playing with your children, serving a customer.

The Trappist monk and spiritual writer Thomas Merton (1915-1968) wrote, 'The gate of heaven is everywhere'. Such a faith awareness does not come easily within a materialistic culture which insists that the only reality is what we can see and touch. A more recent threat to faith awareness or what used to be called 'presence of God' is screen addiction which exiles any prospect of sacred spaces for listening to Spirit's whispers about God's presence. In my daily walks, I notice most young people walk with their eyes firmly fixed on the screens of their iPhone rather than the magic of nature all around them. That remark is not a criticism of a younger cyber generation. It's just how it is.

Jesus encouraged us to live fully in the present when he said, *So do not worry about tomorrow for tomorrow will bring worries of its own. Today's trouble is enough for today* (Matthew 6:34). Living for 'now-moments' deepens our levels of consciousness of what is around us and within us, a spiritual mindfulness. Jesus urged his followers to look around them, *Consider the ravens.... Consider the lilies ...* (Luke 12:24, 27). A faith perspective holds that the Spirit is present at our workplace, in the home, playing with our children, visiting a sick relative, watching TV or surfing through our iPad, laughing and crying.

Jesus used the symbol of bread, a staple food for ordinary people, to tell us who he is, *I am the bread of life. Whoever comes to me will never be hungry* (John 6:35). What could be more 'everyday' than bread and enjoying a meal? The art and practice of focused *gazing* empower us to connect with people and events around us. Why does the more recent (2011) translation of Mass begin with, 'And with your spirit' instead of what was the previous liturgical response, 'And also with you'? As the faith community assembles for Mass, one would hope that God is with our whole beings ('you') not with the dualism of our 'spirit' only!

Jesus challenges us to *Keep awake* (Mark 14:38). The 'Buddha' in Sanskrit means 'I am awake'. Jesus taught about his Dream, the reign of God, using everyday examples to explain the Dream. Metaphors such as flowers in the field, birds in a tree, dishonest employers, shepherds, travellers, forgiving parents, seeds growing, all are images of ordinary life features. illuminating images about the reign of God. According to Jesus, *the Kingdom of God is among you* (Luke 17:21). The late medieval mystic Meister Eckhart (1260-c1329) reminded us that, 'God is at home; it is we who have gone out for a walk' (for quotes of Meister Eckhart, see Fox, M. *Meditations with Meister Eckhart* 1983).

WE ARE ALL CALLED TO MAKE THE WORLD BETTER

According to the Talmud (primary source of Jewish law and theology), 'It is not your obligation to complete your work but you are not at liberty to quit it'. Applying this statement from the Talmud to Christian living, Christians are enjoined through their baptism to do something about the Dream of Jesus, the reign of God. They don't have to fulfil all the imperatives of the Dream but they cannot be excused from doing something positive about the Dream through the utilisation of their birth gifts. Our birth gifts have been given to us, not just for our personal benefits, but for the common good, *To each is given the manifestation of the Spirit for the common good* (1 Corinthians 12: 7).

Through baptism, we become members of the Body of Christ. Our birth gifts are now integral parts of the Body of Christ. According to Paul, *Now you are the body of Christ and individually members of it* (1 Corinthians 12:27). As Jesus began his ministry of preaching and healing (see Mark 1:40-42), so Christians as members of the Body of Christ utilise their birth gifts for this same mission of proclamation and healing.

As we grow older, we become more aware that we have just one short precious life. If, towards the twilight of my life, I consider that my life has made the world around me a little bit better in kindness, love and justice, then that indeed is a good life (note the Jewish *Tikkun Olam:* 'acts of kindness to repair the world'). To live a life without wholesome meaning is to walk a treadmill that leads to a nowhere of despair. When I see media reports of people who have committed serious crime, I sometimes reflect that, 'There, but for the grace of

God, go I' and also a real sadness that this person has made such bad choices for their one life. 'If only...'

GOD IN EVERYDAY HAPPENINGS

Nurturing the presence of God in everyday life does not mean trying to think holy thoughts while changing a baby's nappy or cooking a meal. We may begin our day while making our bed with a simple prayer, 'Help me this day to make the world a better place'. God's presence may not always be some action for kindness but just allowing silence to wrap around us. Perhaps that's not possible with the early morning demands of getting children off to school.

Much of living everyday spirituality is not by spoken words but a deep awareness of the Presence within a silence of the heart, *Be still, and know that I am God* (Psalm 46:10). Within this stillness, we experience a sense of oneness with everyone and everything around us. The mystic Mechtild of Magdeburg (1212-1282) described this oneness:

> *The day of my spiritual awakening*
> *was the day I saw and knew.*
> *I saw all things in God*
> *and God in all things.*

Everyday spirituality does not happen by chance or because we think being spiritual is a good idea. The Spirit works through our own efforts to lead a more spirit-centred life. We have to strive to deepen our spirituality by setting aside spaces for intentional prayer, reading and commitment to the wellbeing of others. A simple act of kindness flows out of a compassionate heart that is fashioned by love.

We also learn to live with the spiritual loneliness of being seemingly deserted by God in the 'dark night of the soul'. Sometimes, our only prayer is a plea of anguish, 'Oh God, why have you forsaken me in this time when I need you so much!'(see Mark 15:34). Our suffering times are invitations to let the healing power of God's love grace the pain of separation, loss of loved ones, crippling anxiety or physical disability.

Our responses to failure and our sinfulness are opportunities for redemptive grace. Through the integration of faith and life experiences, we allow God's presence to infuse every phase of our lives. The social isolation of our neighbour may be our first priority for compassion rather than the famine in Yemen. Kindness becomes second nature to us when we intuitively reach out to others. The face of everyday spirituality may be facilitating social cohesion in our local communities.

We experience the room of Every Day Spirituality when we open the door and invite Jesus to come in to sit with us to engage in intimate conversations (Revelation 3:20).

In the 14th century *Cloud of Unknowing*, the anonymous author wrote, *I encourage you to make experience, not knowledge your aim. Knowledge often leads to arrogance, but this humble feeling never lies to you.*

The place of reality is the invitation to grace. The more fully we become human, the more godlike we become.

PERSONAL RESPONSES

GROUP CONVERSATION STARTERS

If you wish to discuss your views of the room with a friend:

1. *What question would you ask of the author if he were present?*
2. *What question aroused your interest in the text?*
3. *What question was provoked by uncertainty or disagreement with part of the text?*
4. *What question arose with a sense of delight or agreement with what you read?*
5. *What further questions have arisen through reading the text of this room?*

DOOR TO ROOM 2
THE UNIVERSE STORY

Let us open the door of Room Two and enter the room of the Universe Story

How might our Christian faith be fully integrated within the whole web of life in the universe?

BIOCENTRISM NOT ANTROCENTRISM

Much of past Christian theology was like a preoccupation of looking at a mirror of self and gazing at the reflections of our faith beliefs about humanity, God and saving one's soul. This self focus may be called 'anthropocentrism' which means that the human person is the centre of all things. One of the exciting developments in contemporary theology and spirituality is opening a window and looking out of the self-room window to observe the sky, the vast cosmos, stars, planets, plants and animals while reflecting on the amazing story of the evolution of the universe. Instead of confining God to a closed room of our humanity, we open another door and walk into a new room of the sunshine and storms of creation.

The concept of 'biocentrism' situates the human person, not as separate from the cosmos, but firmly intertwined within the pulsating energies of the biosphere. All theology and spirituality then become eco-centric (ecologically centred). How can theology and spirituality

NOT be eco-centric since the origins and nature of the human person are integral to the very essence of all life in the universe? According to Thomas Aquinas (1225-1274), 'If we get creation wrong, we get God wrong'.

THE WONDER OF THE CREATION STORY

Just consider that about 13.7 billion years ago, there was an extraordinary explosion of energy, the Big Bang or Flaring Forth of light and matter which originated our universes and us. Everything that has ever been created: every plant, person, bird, tree, mountain, sea, animal and species was contained within that first explosive energy. Reflecting on this wondrous event surely leads us to a profound sense of awe or, in the words of the author Judy Cannato, an experience of 'radical amazement' (see Cannato, J. *Radical Amazement: Contemplative Lessons from Black Holes, Supernovas, and other Wonders of the Universe*). In 1929, the astrophysicist Edwin Hubble discovered that this primal expansion of the universe continues and we now know that the expansion is accelerating at a faster rate than was previously researched. Perhaps we might actually live in a cosmic realm of not one but multi-universes, always in outwards motion.

Following the initial burst of energy, the evolution of the universe (s) unfolded - particles, atoms, galaxies, stars, supernova explosions, planets including our earth, oceans, emergence of life forms, births and extinctions and eventually hominids and then us. What an awesome 13.7 billion years that continue today in new, evolving life forms!

About 4.4 billion years ago, the earth appeared and the first cells of life emerge at four billion years ago. Photosynthesis (3.9 billion years ago) allowed life to be generated. Much later, a series of cosmic eras evolve such as the Cambrian era (542 million years ago), Devonian era (395 million years ago), Carboniferous era (350 million years ago), Permian (256 million years ago), Triassic era (235 million years ago),

Jurassic (150 million years ago) and then, finally, after other past eras, our own time now which is evolving into who knows what?

As we enter this room of the Universe Story and gaze around, we become more aware that the God of Christian faith is a Divine Energy, a Ground of Being, the Ultimate Reality, a Great Spirit who has initiated an abundant creation. This Creator God abides within the web of life in every dimension of creation. Through our reflections and study of the cosmic story of evolution, we reverence the mystery of the Cosmic God who will not be entombed into prisons of inflexible permanent doctrines. A little god can never be reconciled with the expansive Divinity of an evolving creation.

We can see more of the universe at night than we can during the day. On a clear night sky while gazing at the overarching canopy of blinking stars, do we spend the night worrying about whether it is lawful according to church teachings, if our divorced and remarried friend should or should not go to communion? How big is our God?

IMAGINATION AND THE UNIVERSE

How do we cope with envisaging a universe when, for example, we seek to comprehend or even begin to imagine that:

Most galaxies contain about 100 billion stars.

There are at least 100 billion galaxies.

In the Milky Way, there are 17 billion earth-size planets.

Dark matter and dark energy comprise about 94% of the universe and we know only about 6% of matter. Black holes have now been photographed (2019).

Modern cosmology and imagination are doors into the wonder of the universe. The magnificent Mind of the universe is a mysterious energy that links all the intricate secrets of nature – the unfolding seasons of the year, the birthing, growths and deaths of animals, birds, trees and plants, the movements of sea currents and climate changes, the haunting singing of whales, earthquakes and volcanoes. In the quantum vacuum (QV), all basic fundamental reality, including us, resides there, pulsing with energy (Delio, 2015, 57). Everything in the Mind of the universe is interrelated (see Wohlleben 2017, Ch 2).

The Dutch-American biologist Frans De Waal, one of the world's expert in primate behaviour, believes that language is the only capacity that is uniquely human which separates humans from primates (see De Waal, F. *Mama's Last Hug: Animal Emotions and What they Teach Us about Ourselves*). We live within the intricate and wonderful patterns of energy. According to the medieval monk St Bonaventure (1221-1274), 'Every grain of sand reflects God's energy'. For those of a religious faith, the Mind is the impulse of a Divine Source, the Ground of Being and the Great Spirit, energising the universe.

A study of the story of religion illustrates how regularly religious authorities trap their gods into prisons of doctrinal conformity and minute idols of prohibitions. All too often the Divine Energy of the vast cosmic spaces is reduced by religions to whether it is a venial sin to break a fast or drink from a cup touched by an unbeliever. A church, for example, that does not permit rituals for the burial of a gay partner can hardly be a church faithful to the wonder of an expansive graced creation with its inclusive depths of God's mercy. The God of this awesome creation is infinitely grander than an act of homophobic discrimination.

According to the 13th century Persian poet Rumi,

Stop acting so small.
You are the universe in ecstatic motion.

For Christians, the Christ story belongs to the whole cosmic story of God's revelation, not just the revelation of God in Jesus 2000 years ago. The first great Incarnation happened 13.7 billion years ago. God brought into being the 'flesh' of the evolutionary universe. The universe was the first expression of God's self-giving and self-communication.

In the light of modern science and cosmology, it is increasingly difficult to engage in meaningful contemporary theology divorced from the story of the universe. The ancient three tiered view of heaven above, earth here and underworld below as taught by the Greco-Roman astronomer Ptolemy (110-170 CE) has long been consigned to scientific history. God is not 'up there in heaven' but 'in here within us and creation'. We are conditioned to think this way with the refrains in prayer and liturgy such as, 'Our Father who art in heaven'.

There is wisdom in the story about a preacher with a group of Christian and Hindu children. He asked them, 'Where is God or the Divine One?' The Christian children pointed to the sky while the Hindu children pointed to their hearts.

The assertion that, according to Newtonian physics, matter is a series of independent atoms has been supplanted by quantum physics that shows that all matter is focused relational energy. Newtonian physics was ordered and predictable. Matter was composed of atoms like a series of building blocks. Quantum physics is characterised by uncertainty, random, relationships and unpredictability. Morphogenetic fields direct forms of systems towards other members of the same species in a phenomenon called by Rupert Sheldrake 'morphic resonance'. The morphogenetic fields allow spiritual energy of God in Jesus to move across space and time to those who are attuned to the gospel. The Christ energy of the Eucharist is carried by morphic resonance across space and 2000 years to us at Mass following the command of Jesus in the Last Supper, *Do this in remembrance of me* (Luke 22:21).

Ilya Prigogine's (1917-2003) theory of Emergence proposed how more complex systems evolve after the original system falls into disorder. How does a church reconcile past traditions of unchanging order and conformity with the evolutionary, unpredictable quantum world? How does the church affirm core beliefs in the Good News yet be open to possibilities of new wisdoms emerging or, in the words of the theologian John Haught, 'the lure of the future' which beckons us to new horizons? (see Delio, 2015, 142). What might be the character of future Christianity? Will all future theology be situated within an 'eco-centric' world view?

Our images of divinity cannot be restricted to a closed box of metaphors that were formed during a 2000 year old epoch of pre-modern frame that married Christian images about God with Greek philosophy. We are now more attuned to an evolving Divine Energy, the *ruach* or Great Spirit of a 13.7 billion year old creative Source. To move towards a union with God is to become more aware of living within the interconnectedness of all things in creation.

The 12th century mystic Hildegard of Bingen wrote about this interconnectedness, 'Everything that is in heavens, in the earth, and under the earth is penetrated with connectedness, with relatedness'. Scientists tell us how the amazing process of photosynthesis happened about 3.7 billion years ago when the light from the sun began to generate the first forms of life on the planet earth. Jesus said, *I am the light of the world. Whoever follows me will never walk in darkness but will have the light of life* (John 8:12). As the light of photosynthesis brings life to planet earth, Christian faith teaches that the light of Jesus brings God's revelation to humankind.

Where do you most experience wonder in creation?

THE EARTH IS OUR HOME

For centuries, most Christians regarded the earth as a testing place to see if we were worthy of heaven. The universe was a mere backdrop to the drama of salvation on centre stage. Today, we now know that we live our Christian faith within a very different scientific world view. The story of the universe is our story because we all are children of stardust. Like Jesus, my very being has evolved from the star dust emanating from the explosions of supernovas. I am part of the intricate web of life in every aspect of creation. Hence, I am challenged to do whatever I can to enhance planetary health. The earth is truly our home with all its intricate wonders of life, death and rebirth. Are we serious about creative living within the wondrous cosmic story?

When walking my dog Darcy around Eildon Hill, I often look down on the hillside covered with an array of trees, flowers and tangled undergrowth and, reflecting on the millions of evolutionary generations, wish to call out to bounteous nature on display, 'Why are you here? Where did you come from? Tell me your story?' What an amazing mystery it is to reflect on how over those four hundred millions years since the Devonian period, these trees, flowers and plants ended up on this hillside!

Every single person can do something to care for the earth, whether it be limiting the use of plastics, promoting solar power, switching off lights not in use, joining community ecological groups, planting trees, gardening, promoting renewable energy sources. One of my lasting joys was planting hundreds of rainforest trees at our Samford acreage. St Francis of Assisi (1182-1226) was told in a vision, 'Go and repair my home'. His mission of 'repairing our earthen home' is our earth mission now.

Humanity has to make rather dramatic adaptations in how we live to restore the wellbeing of the planet. Global warming must be kept below 1.5 degrees Celsius (see *Global Warming*. United Nations Published Summary 8 October 2018). Rising sea levels threaten low lying countries. Climate change is happening much more rapidly than earlier forecasts predicted. One rubbish truck worth of plastic is dumped into our oceans every <u>minute.</u> Two billion people do not have regular access to drinkable water. Only a real change in how we live will save our planet from ecological devastation. (See IPBES global biodiversity assessment May 2019 indicating unprecedented deterioration of planetary ecosystems.) Do we have the will and courage to modify our living styles? Are we open to a New Story for how our Christian faith is taught and lived?

The First Peoples of each country, such as the Aboriginal and Torres Strait people of Australia, the Maori people in New Zealand, the Native American Indians have much wisdom to share about planetary health if only we would listen to them. Nature herself is a wise teacher. According to Job, *But ask the animals, and they will teach you; the birds of the air, and they will tell you, ask the plants of the earth, and they will teach you* (12:7-8). How do I live with the paradoxes of nature – the myriad colours of an orchid garden with the brutality of a lunging crocodile to snatch a thirsty impala, the thrill of surfing waves with the towering destructive waves of a tsunami?

Nature is a confusing mix of breathtaking beauty and capricious devastation, flood and drought, the joy and anguish of nature's paradoxes. The dark side of nature is, to quote the poet Tennyson, 'red in tooth and claw'. Life and death are inherent in the cycle of nature. Suffering and extinction are as integral to the dynamics of the universe as is evolutionary growth. At least 96% of all species that have ever appeared on earth have become extinct in the five Great Dyings since the Cambrian period (480 – 420 million years ago).

We are now probably living in the onset of a Sixth Dying, the *Antropocene* era, where multiple extinctions and ecological denigration are largely caused by human vandalism (see Christian, D. *Origin Story: A Big History of Everything, chapter* 11: '*The Anthropocene: Threshold 8*'). In the evolutionary story of the universe, for the very first time, one

species (humans) is having a major impact on the course of evolution
to the detriment of all other species in the biosphere.

The words of the poet William Blake evoke our intimacy with
the earth:

> *To see a world in a grain of sand*
> *And a heaven in a wildflower,*
> *Hold infinity in the palm of your hand*
> *And eternity in an hour.*

Auguries of Innocence

RELIGIOUS FAITH AND CREATION

Our Christian faith is celebrated within a perspective of a time
frame of 13.7 billion years, not simply the 2000 year old story since
the coming of Jesus as the Christ. According to Daniel O'Leary, 'To
explore the meaning of Jesus Christ in evolution, it is helpful to keep
several ideas in mind. The first is that creation and incarnation are
not two separate events but one process of God's self-giving and self-
communication. When we talk about Incarnation, we are also talking
about creation' (2018, 48). The beginning of John's Gospel (John 1:1-
14) is a parallel to the beginning of creation told as in the Genesis (1:1-
2): *and the Word became flesh and lived among us* (John 1:14) is the divine
echo of, *In the beginning when God created the heavens and the earth*
(Genesis 1:1).

In the encyclical letter on ecology and climate *Laudato si* (2015),
Pope Francis called on all peoples to address the issue of planetary
health. For a Christian, eco-ethics is not an option for discipleship
but an imperative for living out the implications of our baptism (see
Laudato si, Chapter 6 *Ecological Education and Spirituality*). Faithful to
beliefs of the Incarnation, Christians are committed to affirm their
humanity within the biosphere of creation. The concept of 'deep

ecology' emphasises the rights of all living things to survive and flourish. Humans are not lords of the universe but are creatures within the great evolutionary cycle of birth, life, death, rebirth/extinction.

According to Genesis, the first Covenant, symbolised by a rainbow, was between God, humanity and creation (9:13). The 'cosmotheandric' vision of reality as explained by the interreligious theologian Raimon Panikkar (1918-2010) described the interconnection of the divine (*theos*) human (*anthropos*) and cosmos (*cosmos*) (Panikkar, R. *The Cosmotheandric Experience: Emerging Religious Consciousness* Beijing. Cultural Publishing House, 2006). All theology and cosmology are interrelated. Until recently, especially during the previous four hundred years of Christian theology, one of the three partners in the first covenant viz. creation (*cosmos*), was regularly consigned to the attic of theological irrelevance.

We each have our own approaches to being in kinship with nature. A blessing before meals may be a sacred pause time to reflect on a bounteous earth and the marvel of how evolution has delivered these vegetables on our table. I celebrate each morning how nature allows me to live for another day as I honour the earth and the Great Spirit for its life-giving oxygen enabling me to breathe. The Divine Breath or *nephesh* or the Enabler Great Spirit generates all life in creation (Genesis 1:2) (see Edwards, D. *Partaking of God: Trinity, Evolution, and Ecology*, 24-26).

A Jewish name of YHWH was not expressed by articulation of a word but a sequence of breathings. Slow breathing intake for the breathing of 'YH' and then slow breathing out for 'WH'. Yoga, tai'chi and stress- diminishing exercises regulate breathing as an essential feature of such activities. John's Gospel associates breathing with the energy of the Spirit, *When he had said this, he breathed on them and said to them, 'Receive the Holy Spirit'* (20:22).

A Sufi mystic once described this breathing as,

'All is contained in the Divine Breath, like the day in the morning's dawn'.

Every person will choose and act on their ways of fostering kinship with creation. Surveys among a younger generation indicate a strong endorsement to action to address climate change. How inspiring it is to witness the 16 year old Greta Thunberg from Sweden travelling the world, pleading with political leaders to do something to address the crisis emanating from climate change. And there is Nemonte, a young mother from the Waorani Nation in Ecuador, leading the fight to save the Amazon forests. As followers of Christ and citizens of the earth community, our baptism demand nothing less than positive participation in earth membership (see *Laudato si,* 218). Eco-spirituality is not simply *doing* something to enhance nature but creatively *being* within this magnificent web of life.

To what degree is your spirituality fashioned by a sense of kinship with the earth community?

What better way of concluding this room of the Universe Story than quoting the Aboriginal leader Narritjin Yirrkala, *We belong to the ground. It is our power and we must stay close to it or maybe we will get lost.*

Let us open the door of Room Two, the Universe Story and celebrate our kinship in creation.

PERSONAL RESPONSES

GROUP CONVERSATION STARTERS

If you wish to discuss your views of the room with a friend:

1. *What question would you ask of the author if he were present?*
2. *What question aroused your interest in the text?*
3. *What question was provoked by uncertainty or disagreement with part of the text?*
4. *What question arose with a sense of delight or agreement with what you read?*
5. *What further questions have arisen through reading the text of this room?*

DOOR TO ROOM 3
HUMANS AND RELIGION

Let us open the door of Room Three and enter the room of Humans and Religion.

How does our humanity mesh with religious beliefs and practices?

THE EVOLUTION OF HUMANS

A core Christian belief is the Incarnation, *And the Word became flesh and lived among us* (John 1:14). The human narrative thus is central to the Jesus as the Christ story.

The evolution of humans is a very late development in the 13.7 billion year old story of the universe. Emerging out of hydrogen, oxygen, carbon and nitrogen, stardust from explosions of supernovas, palaeontologists propose that, about seven million years ago, some form of hominids appeared. There are various theories about the origins of our own species, *homo sapiens.*

Over the millions of years, various forms of hominids merged and then became extinct. Palaeontologists have discovered fossil remains in Kenya that show that there were at least two lineages of the human species in East Africa about two million years ago. A more recent version of hominids was the Neanderthals who only became extinct as recently as 23,000 years ago. Another species of hominids, the Denisovans have left their genetic imprint on our DNA.

About 150,000 years ago, *homo sapiens* suddenly appeared as the dominant and then the exclusive species of the hominids. Our species exhibited powers of self-reflection, language, art and consciousness. With the rapid advances now in global technology, genetics and space travel, perhaps we are moving towards a newer trans-human form of hominids, especially if, in future times, settlements are made on other planets such as Mars. Given the evolutionary nature of all things in a globally connected universe, almost certainly there will be another form of *homo sapiens* as *homo universalis*.

Although the summary of salient features of the evolutionary human destiny given above is generally scientifically endorsed, it is noted that in a USA 2 June 2014 Gallup poll, 42% of the population believe that God created humans as they are now within the previous ten thousand years (quoted in Delio 2015, 55).

The Christian faith is a very recent happening in the evolution of the human species and even within the story of religions.

GOD AND HUMANS

The biblical account of the creation of the human person illuminates how humans were composed of earth (*adamah*: the earth) (Genesis 2:18-24). Adam needed a 'helper' (Hebrew: *ezer*), note, not as an inferior feminine person, but as a strong companion to rescue her partner from his 'aloneness' (Genesis 2:18). The Hebrew *ezer* is derived from two root words meaning 'rescue' and 'strong'. The translation of 'ezer' to 'helper' is a poor translation suggesting subordinate and patriarchal. The Divine Energy breathed life into these beings. Humans are very close in their DNA to some animals, birds and nature generally. We share 98.8% of our DNA with chimps, 50% of our DNA with bananas. Our DNA, like those of nature, orientates us towards cooperation and mutuality rather than competition and domination. One of the fascinating observations by the world renowned primatologist Frans De Waal in his book *Mama's Last Hug* is how animals are very willing to help one another, even to the point of delaying food rewards until others are given some food also.

The word 'religion' (Latin *religare*, 'binding together') speaks about connecting us with all things and bringing a deeper meaning to humankind than living solely for material possessions. Archaeologists have uncovered evidence from very early times in human history of an association with the numinous in nature and an awareness of the Great Spirit. The First Peoples assumed the reality of the presence of divine forces in nature all around them. Ancient burial sites illustrated religious rituals. Cave art portrayed the intimate connection between nature, humans and divine forces.

The Axial epoch (800 BCE – 300 BCE) witnessed an evolutionary leap in philosophical and religious thinking with the emergence of Confucianism and Taoism in China, Buddhism and Hinduism in India, monotheism of Judaism and Zoroaster in the Middle East and the philosophies of Greece. The three monotheistic religions of Judaism, Christianity and Islam developed patriarchal and hierarchal traditions within their religious cultures.

The history of the emergence of religions describes how the development of settled rather than nomadic hunter tribal living promoted intermediaries between divine spirits and the people. A priestly class evolved that would determine rituals, worship, beliefs and moral codes. In the Christian religion, the rise of a clerical caste, especially after the fourth century, disempowered early Christians by reducing them to a spiritually dependent lay state. As the story of religion attests, a danger for all religions is that intermediaries between God or gods and people gradually assume the role of gatekeepers who specify who is worthy or not worthy of salvation into paradise or nirvana.

There is much evidence to suggest that some expressions of spirituality or link with some form of divinity are deeply embedded within the human psyche. The French philosopher Blaise Pascal (1623-1662) described this orientation, 'There is a God shape vacuum in the heart of each person which cannot be satisfied by any created thing but only by God'. Our human DNA would seem to indicate that a sense of transcendence is integral to our humanity. According to Genesis, *So God created humankind in his image, in the image of God he created them; male and female he created them* (1:27).

Perhaps a more authentic way of describing the human species is *homo religiosus* Being religious does not necessarily imply that a person belongs to a religion with doctrines and creeds. Rather it describes the propensity towards a spiritual vision of life that gives meaning to the perennial question, 'What does it mean to live, given the fact that one day I will die?' A caution here would alert us about how the rise in those professing atheism, especially in Western countries, raises all kinds of questions about the assumption that being religious is a given for human DNA.

In your experience of meeting people, do you think most people are basically spiritual in their life vision?

SIN AND THE HUMAN CONDITION

Personal or communal sin is an aberration against wholeness in life and the wider community. The word for 'sin' is derived from the Old German word *sunda* meaning to 'sunder' or 'tear apart'. Sin is tearing us apart from God, others and creation. Another approach for understanding the nature of wrongdoing is to consider the Greek *hamartia* which relates to archery where 'missing the mark' is 'missing the mark' of being wholesome through personal or social sin. The biblical myth of Adam and Eve in the garden describes the prospect of alienation from God as a characteristic of the human condition. Humans can and do make evil choices. Every day, our media is full of reports of the sinfulness of humanity, domestic violence, greed, terrorism, bullying, robbery, duplicity - the depressing list rolls on.

Such explanations about sin seem to make much more sense than describing sin as 'an offense against God'. In the ancient Hebrew Scriptures, the understanding of the devil or Satan was not some kind of fallen angel but as an 'obstruction' to God's will. The phrase 'lead us not into temptation' in the 'Our Father' is a plea that we resist 'obstructions' to God's will and choose instead love and harmony (see Psalm 66:10).

The doctrine of original sin was never part of the official church's teaching during the first four centuries (see Mahoney, J. *Christianity in Evolution.* ' Dispensing with Original Sin', 51-57). Teachings about original sin sought to explain the global presence of sin in the world and the problem of human choices which denigrate the human person and the integrity of creation. The doctrine of original sin taught that humanity has inherited a collective guilt as a consequence of the sin (sic) of Adam and Eve. The 16th century church reformer John Calvin wrote about the 'total depravity' of humanity.

Today, the emphasis in our birthing is more on the blessedness of coming into the world rather than beginning life in a state of inherited alienation from God's grace. In the words of Matthew Fox, 'original blessing' rather than 'original sin' describes life beginnings for people (see Fox, M. *Original Blessing: A Primer in Creation Spirituality*). As the evolutionary story of humanity unfolds why would we believe that people begin life morally flawed? No studies in palaeontology or anthropology have ever uncovered any evidence about an inherited morally flawed nature in humans. Certainly early Christianity, Judaism and Islam have no such beliefs about a doctrine of original sin.

The human paradox of blessings/sinfulness was highlighted for me once when working in the Highlands of Papua New Guinea. When I concluded my conference on the teachings of Jesus and was leaving the small hall, I noticed a utility slowly passing by with two dead bodies in the back of a utility – victims killed in a local tribal war. Right there in front of me was the stark evidence of how the Jesus message of reconciliation which we had just considered in the hall was contradicted by the murderous consequences of violent tribal conflict. Such moral yin/yang is the story of humankind. While humanity is not inherently morally flawed, we cannot deny the reality of sinfulness. Just reflect on the barbarity of Auschwitz and the Holocaust.

The prospect and hope of redemption await the experience of a heart open to grace and reconciliation. While there has never been a time of perfection in the evolution of the human species (the Eden principle), for those of religious faith, there is the gradual desire for a profound relationships with the source of all life, a Divine Energy of love. In Christian belief, the dying and resurrection of Jesus as the Christ is the archetypal image of this evolving movement. We all carry seeds of resurrection within us. However, it seems there has to be some form of dying to enable these resurrection seeds to germinate into a new flowering of life. The iconic symbol of the cross in Christianity images both the reality of suffering and sinfulness with a hope of resurrection.

HUMANS AND THE QUEST FOR LIFE

The quest for life is a driving impulse in the human condition. The teachings of Jesus focused on the attainment of a fullness of life – life for self, others, creation and experiencing the life of God (grace): *I came that they may have life, and have it abundantly* (John 10:10). God's revelation in Jesus was and is to show how humanity and divinity may be brought together, empowering humanity to live holistically within the web of life in creation. Christianity is lived authentically when it enhances the wellbeing of people and creation. Doctrines in Christianity are expressed as doorways into the Mystery room of God as the Ground of Being. Doctrines are lighthouses to illuminate religious truths but are not definitive statements about the nature of God whose identity can never be fully captured by language. In a certain sense we can only really talk about God in metaphors.

The first commandment in the Jewish/Torah tradition forbids 'having strange gods before me'. A danger for all religions, especially creedal religions, is to fall into idolatry by becoming fixated through a worship of idols such as canon law, purity laws and Sabbath observance to the detriment of the gospel. Jesus furiously attacked such idols in his own religion by overturning tables in the Temple and challenging leaders about purity laws and Sabbath observance (Matthew 23).

Questions such as the following consider conflicting values between canon law and the common good: 'Is the seal of confession to be considered more important than the welfare of a child when a person has confessed paedophile acts (see Crothers 90)?', 'Are the laws of the church superior to the integrity of people and civil law?' Perhaps the reintroduction of the Third Rite of Reconciliation might address the dilemma of reconciling the seal of confession commitment with the imperative of legal disclosure.

Death is an integral feature of all life forms including the human person. For a Christian death and a transformative resurrection are two essential dimensions of what it means to be human. Through death, humans move to an alternative state of being. Diverse religions and life philosophies have various narratives to describe the journey into after-life.

We don't really know what happens after death although a religious faith offers certain beliefs about after-life. Perhaps the deep Inner Self of our being emerges out of the decomposition of the bodily and Ego Self. Death is a transition into a transformative state of Inner or Deep Self, the essence of our being. Some years ago, at an internment ritual of the ashes of a relative, I experienced a vision of that person standing directly above us looking down peacefully upon us. I could clearly recognise my relative but he was in an illuminated state. Many people have such visions (Nowotny-Keane, E. *Amazing Encounters: Direct Communication from the After-Life*). The vision was a startling reminder to me that the numinous world is all around us although we rarely have glimpses of it.

For a Christian and possibly for others of religious faiths, there is a belief of how death is a passing over of the Inner or True Self into the embrace of God or Divine Presence as the Source of Love (heaven). Hell is some form of impediment to this transition. For a Christian, the resurrection of Jesus as the Christ is the exemplar and archetype of our own resurrections of passing over to another transformed form of our Being-Self. The doctrines of 'Communion of Saints' and 'Mystical Body' are evocative images of the interconnections between our earthly existences and the realm of the numinous in a resurrected Christ.

Every person is enjoined to contribute to the wellbeing of others, seeking a more just and fair world as well as active participation in creation. Religion has the potential for humans to discover a universal unity of connectedness within the essence of life in creation. Sadly, history attests that religion has all too often been a source of malevolent strife and alienation between different religious groups and creeds.

Religion has also been and is now a major source for good with its spirituality, pastoral care, arts, culture and especially offering positive life orientations and support within the paradoxes of life. St Irenaeus (130-202), one of the eminent Church Fathers in the early church, summed up the exaltation of humanity in God when he wrote,

'For the glory of God is the living person and the life of a person is the vision of God (*Against Heresies* Book 4, Chapter 34, Section 7) (see also Ephesians 3:18-19).

Rapid scientific advances in genetics, artificial Intelligence (AI), cloning and the influence of extensive utilisation of cyber technology in brain functions portend a dramatic evolution in the very nature of the human person. What is neuroscience telling us about changing patterns of how our brain functions? Are we witnessing the emergence of a trans-human or post-human person? If so, what are the future implications for religion and the human person?

For the first time in the history of humanity's intellectual evolution, ordinary people's spoken and written word can flash across the whole world with a press 'send' from their iPad or iPhone. How does this revolution in human global connectivity impact on the Christ story? Does absorption or even addiction with accessing social media limit face-to-face relationships? What are the implications for communal togetherness and social cohesion if most of our friends are Facebook friends only?

There are many challenges to the condition of the human person today. On one level there are enormous advances in understandings about the physical body, health, psychological wellbeing and sexuality. Wisdoms gained from the social sciences, anthropology, neuroscience, psychology and sociology offer helpful insights into the human character. Many global disease threats have been eliminated. On the other hand there is a scandalous disparity in wealth distribution and serious starvation. Mental health issues are reaching alarming proportions especially among the young in Western countries. A study by Oxford and McGill universities found that people who smoked cannabis before the age of 18 were at a 37% more risk in developing serious depression before the age of 32. Due to the increment in robots and AI applications in business and industry, there is an estimate that, in the UK alone, about thirty million workers during the next twenty years will no longer be employed in their current workplaces. Robotics raise significant ethical questions especially about the ways robotic operations impact on human relations and society generally.

With all the benefits of social media, one of its downsides is the challenge of addictions in spending hours of watching screens instead of getting out into parks and doing exercise. By the age of eight, it is estimated that a child in Australia has spent one whole year watching a screen (International research from the Association of Play Industries). It would appear that this screen addiction is impacting on the emotional and religious functions of the brain to access religious experiences. 'Screen sabbaths' are encouraged for those addicted to excessive screen viewing. We might even plead for a limit to the number of 'selfies' taken each day! An analysis of internet data estimates that 30% of all data transferred on the internet is pornography.

The lure and even addiction of the social media is a factor in enticing children away from healthy play outdoors. We are witnessing the rise of a 'no play' generation (Hyano Moser from Nature Play Queensland). Instagram can lead to a state of living by comparisons and reinforcing low self-esteem: 'He or she looks better than me'; 'They go for overseas holidays and I am stuck here'; 'I wish I had her figure but I'm so revoltingly fat'. Cyber bullying is also a growing menace to the more vulnerable, especially in the teenage group.

However, the negatives of social media are to be balanced against the enormous social benefits of communications, recreation, critical role in crisis situations, dissemination of helpful alerts, contacts, business and industry, access to information through Google, instant messages sent and received over long distances.

The dignity of a person, made in the image and likeness of God, stands firm against denigrations arising from social media and robotics. According to Paul, our bodies are sacred, *Or do you not know that your body is a temple of the Holy Spirit within you* (1 Corinthians 6:19).

How do you critically evaluate the pros and cons of our humanity in our world today?

LOVE AND LIFE'S MEANING FOR HUMANS

The French mystic and palaeontologist Pierre Teilhard de Chardin (1881-1955) offered an optimistic vision for humanity. He proposed that love-energy was the core impulse in the evolution of the universe, moving towards an Omega point. According to Teilhard de Chardin, *Love is the most universal, the most tremendous and the most mysterious of the cosmic forces...* (Pierre Teilhard de Chardin, *Human Energy*, trans. J. M. Cohen. New York: William Collins, 1969. 72). If we agree with Teilhard's thesis, then the key to open door Three into the room of Humans and Religion is the power of love to unlock the potential of humanity as co-creators, *If we love one another, God lives in us, and his love is perfected in us* (1 John 4:12).

We are encouraged to care for our own wellbeing through exercise, dieting, plenty of laughter, a positive view of life, nurturing relationships, kinship with nature and care for others. Modern technology does have a downside but it has also brought enormous benefits to virtually every facet of modern living such as travel, elimination of many diseases, food harvesting, communications, 3D technology, forest regeneration, health and education. If only technology could be harnessed to alleviate poverty and hunger in those countries where the majority of people barely survive in basic deprivations!

We grieve for all those whose humanity is diminished by crippling poverty, unjust imprisonment, loneliness and social isolation, refugees; and stricken by disease. As we open the door and enter Room Three of Humans and Religion, we know that religion has the potential to empower humanity towards an 'abundance of life' if each religious tradition is faithful to the core of its mission.

Consider St Augustine's (354-430) advice in his 'Sermon on Love' – 'Love and do what you will'. Perhaps Francis of Assisi has the most succinct summary of our humanity, 'What I am before God is what I am'.

Do you not know that you are God's temple and that God's Spirit dwells in you? (1 Corinthians 3:16).

Personal Responses

Group Conversation Starters

If you wish to discuss your views of the room with a friend:

1. *What question would you ask of the author if he were present?*
2. *What question aroused your interest in the text?*
3. *What question was provoked by uncertainty or disagreement with part of the text?*
4. *What question arose with a sense of delight or agreement with what you read?*
5. *What further questions have arisen through reading the text of this room?*

DOOR TO ROOM 4
THE MYSTERY OF GOD

Let us open the door of Room Four and enter the room on the Mystery of God.

When you use the word 'God', what is your image/understanding of 'God'?

NAMING GOD

All religious believers have some images of a Divine Presence such as Great Spirit, Friend, Judge, Remote Supreme Force, Lover, Father, Braham, Healer, Mother, Source of Energy, Shiva, Parent, Lord, Altjira, Cosmic Creator. Our earliest images of God appear to be shaped by relationships with parental figures or significant adults. I find it interesting to note a number of writings on religion now use some code word such as G-D to refer to a Divine Presence or God (see Sanguin, B. *The Way of the Wind: The Path and Practice of Evolutionary Christian Mysticism*). To such writers the word 'God' is so overladen with agenda that they prefer to use a designation such as 'G_D'. According to Thomas Aquinas, the real nature of God is simply inaccessible to the capacities of the human mind. Perhaps we can only speak about a divinity in images of... 'God is like...'

DIVINE IMAGES

Since the beginning of human consciousness, the question, 'Who or what is god/God or the Great Spirit?' has been posed by tribal groups about the mystery of a divine presence in the natural world. Throughout the thousands of years of human consciousness, various tribal groups and cultures have sought to name the Ultimate Reality, Divine Presence, Ground of Being, God, Allah, Elohim, Krishna, Brahma, Jehovah. Ultimately words will always fail to capture the essence of such a Divine Presence. The First Epistle of John states quite succinctly, *God is love...* (4:16). The medieval mystic Meister Eckhart (1260- c1329) wrote, 'You may call God love. You may call God goodness. But the best name for God is compassion' (see Armstrong, K. *A History of God,* 1999).

It is difficult to describe the Divine Presence in words rather than use metaphors about such a Presence. In the Bible, a popular Hebrew word for God names God as YHWH which is a verb that expresses past, present and future tenses all at once, suggesting the eternal newness of the Divine Presence that was, is and will be. When Moses asked God his (her) name, the answer was enigmatic, *I am who I am* (Exodus 3:14), in other words, 'I will not be confined by you into your belief box. My Presence is beyond the limits of any name you might give me'. The spiritual leader Fr Thomas Keating O.C.S.O (1923-2018) wrote, 'God's first language is silence. Everything else is a translation'.

St Paul issues a warning about those who profess absolute certainty about naming God, *For now we see in a mirror, dimly, but then we will see face to face* (1 Corinthians 13:12). History tells us that when religions specify that they know definitely who God is, there are serious problems about prospects for multi-faith dialogue or inter-faith cooperation. The history of religion is replete with the tragic consequences of religious traditions claiming an exclusive dogmatic ownership of the divine.

Religious fanaticism and bigotry have wrought extreme sufferings on innocent people. According to Karen Armstrong, a world renowned scholar of religion, 'In the West the idea that religion is inherently violent is now taken for granted and seems self-evident' (2014, 1). Monotheistic religions (Judaism, Christianity, Islam) proclaim that they worship one supreme deity (e.g. YHWH, God, Allah) in their own traditions and beliefs. Islam has ninety-nine names or attributes for Allah. Religions such as Hinduism and indigenous religions worship a multitude of sacred deities. How foolish and arrogant it is for any one religion to insist that it and it alone has a tribal monopoly of knowing who God is!

The story of religions tells how feminine and masculine icons are woven into the tapestry of divine images. In the Bible, there is a preponderance of masculine images although there are some allegorical references to God as feminine, mainly in a maternal mode. The language of the liturgy and official church teachings are almost exclusively male and invite future revisions for language inclusivity.

Throughout history, the most persistent enduring images of a divine presence are the images of the Great Spirit and Mother Goddess, manifestations of fertility and divine energy which infuse life within creation and humanity. Most religious groups express their relationships with the Sacred Energy of the Great Spirit through rituals, worship, art, scriptures, music and dancing. With the rise of religions in Egypt, Greece, the Middle East and India, religious worship became more structured. Oral traditions and Scriptures began to describe features of their gods, goddesses and divinities. A persistent motif in images of God or divinity is a belief about the *intervention* God who would 'intervene' for example, to divide the Red Sea for Moses to allow the Israelites to pass through or the *intervention* God who would not allow a beloved friend to die. Jesus did encourage prayers to God to grant us our desires, *Ask and it will be given to you; search and you will find; knock and the door will be opened for you* (Matthew 7:7).

In more recent years, at least in Western countries, those who now profess atheism are on the rise. Atheism proposes a scientific and materialistic worldview that supplants a religious appreciation of humanity's consciousness. For atheists, the world of the gods is relegated to past eras of ignorance and fundamentalism.

Who is God for you? What is your favourite image(s) of God?

REVELATION

The concept of revelation looms large in many religions. How do we know about God? The word 'revelation' suggests the disclosure of something that was previously unknown. In a Christian understanding of revelation, God's special and unique revelation was through the coming of Jesus and his life, death and resurrection. Jesus said to Thomas, *If you know me you will know my Father also* (John 14:7). Jesus experienced God as an intimate *Abba* Father who goes to excessive lengths to embrace outsiders and the marginalised. When we come to know the *Abba* God of Jesus, then we too will encounter this *Abba* God of mercy and compassion.

In more recent times, God's revelation through the wonders of creation has received a recovered prominence. The Church Fathers in early Christianity began to explore how nature reveals God's presence in the world. By the Middle Ages, the Two Books of God – the Book of Nature and the Book of Scripture – were accepted as integral to God's revelation. There is now a growing appreciation of God's revelation that is manifest throughout the whole of creation and every facet of human consciousness.

A positive feature of contemporary religious landscape is attentiveness to listen to the spiritual aspirations of diverse religious traditions. We learn about God through the wisdoms of Judaism, Hinduism, Islam, Indigenous mythologies, Buddhism and Taoism. God's gracious love is universal and not confined to Christians as though Jesus were some kind of tribal possession by the church. In Islam, the Divine Presence as Allah has been revealed through the archangel Gabriel to the Prophet Mohammad. As explained previously (Room One) a grievous aberration in Christianity of the Christ Story has been the thousand year old teaching of the church that 'outside the church there is no salvation' (see *Cantate Domino* 1441).

It seems that we know most about who God is through our life experiences of receiving love and care from our parents, others and nature. I may see the face of God in the face of someone who is wiping away my tears of loss. I may experience a divine Presence in marvelling at the myriad colours of a sunset sky. I may sense the embrace of God by joyful family celebrations. I may feel God's compassion when I watch the gentle pastoral care of a Christian minister.

I may gain insight into the mystery of God through the teachings of the church. I may be swept up emotionally with God's tender mercy when the congregation sings, *You raise me up,* I may also feel a revulsion about God when my best friend is killed in an accident. Emotions about God that well up from the heart may move me more than talks about God.

A perennial question for a 'seeker' is, 'How do we modify or change our perception of who God is?' Is my imaging of God one that is predominantly male? Over the years, I have been personally challenged in my own spiritual journey to complement my previously dominant male perceptions of God with feminine images of the Divine Presence

What is your story about your changing perceptions of God?

THE ONENESS OF GOD

Our images of God are multi-faceted and evolve from a whole array of experiences such as parental relationships, religious formation, witness of people, companionship with nature, suffering, cultural heritages, worship and communal participations. God or a Divine Presence sometimes may seem close to us and at other times far away or even absent. Negative experiences, such as sexual abuse by religious ministers, can evoke hatred of all things connected with God.

Mystics sometimes spoke about the oneness of all things in God as well as the dark night of the soul. The Bible has a whole host of images of God such as Shepherd, Eagle, Wind, Mother, Father, Rock, Living Water and Comforter. Ultimately, we cannot really know who God is through our intellect alone but rather know something of who God is by allowing a *faith sense* of God's love and compassion to graciously touch us.

The mystic Meister Eckhart (c1260 – c1328) described the oneness of God and us:

The knower and the known are one.
Simple people imagine that they should see God
As if he stood there and they here.
This is not so.
God and I, we are one in the knowledge.

For a Christian, a core metaphor of God is Trinity, expressing how the very nature of God as Father, Son and Spirit is a relational God, a Divine Energy of relationships infusing the whole of creation. Quantum physics affirms a relational, interconnected universe. As we grow in love and compassion, we enter more fully into who or what a Trinitarian Divine Presence means. Is my God a Divine Presence of intimate connectedness?

As we open the door and enter Room Four of the Mystery of God, we become more keenly aware of how we may first encounter God not by words about God but by experiences of Divine Love in the faces of people and the wonders of nature.

> *In the beginning when God created the heavens and the earth, the earth was a formless void and darkness covered the face of the deep, while a wind from God swept over the face of the waters* (Genesis 1:1-2).

PERSONAL RESPONSES

GROUP CONVERSATION STARTERS

If you wish to discuss your views of the room with a friend:

1. *What question would you ask of the author if he were present?*
2. *What question aroused your interest in the text?*
3. *What question was provoked by uncertainty or disagreement with part of the text?*
4. *What question arose with a sense of delight or agreement with what you read?*
5. *What further questions have arisen through reading the text of this room?*

Door to Room 5
Meeting Jesus

Let us open the door of Room Five and enter the room of Jesus as the Christ

Who is Jesus for you now?

Life Of Jesus

Jesus (Yeshua or Joshua) is probably the most influential person in human history. He was born in a tiny remote village of Nazareth in northern Galilee, the son of Joseph and Mary. According to the Gospel closest, chronologically, to the life of Jesus, the Gospel of Mark (6:3), Jesus had four brothers (James, Joses, Judas, Simon) and two sisters. We know very little about his childhood days. As a Jewish boy, he would have been circumcised after eight days, celebrated rituals as prescribed by the Torah and initiated into the teachings of the Torah.

About the age of thirty, Jesus had a profound religious experience (Matthew 3:13-17; 4:1-11; Luke 3:21-22) which impelled him into preaching and healing. According to Matthew, the first words of Jesus in preaching were, *Repent, for the kingdom of heaven has come near* (4:17). The word 'repent' is an inadequate translation of the Greek *metanoia* which means to 'move to another mind set'. The driving theme in his preaching was the kingdom of heaven or reign of God (*basileia*: Greek, *malkhuta dishmayya*: Aramaic). Jesus encouraged and enjoined people to move to a higher level of consciousness for living the vision and values of the reign of God.

TEACHINGS OF JESUS

The reign of God portrayed the coming of a new time where, *The last will be first, and the first will be last* (Matthew 20:16). In this new dawning era, God's gracious mercy will be accessible for everyone, social status reversed and turned upside down. In the Jewish world of Jesus, God is king of all creation and God's sovereign rule will last for all time.

Jesus is to inaugurate the kingdom of God as foretold by the prophets. The reign of God was illuminated by miracles of healing and confrontation with the power blocs of religious authorities and Satan. The power of Jesus will overcome evil, *But if it is by the finger of God that I cast out demons, then the kingdom of God has come to you* (Luke 11:20). There were no 'ifs' and 'buts' when Jesus taught. He spoke straight from the heart with authority, *They were astounded by his teaching, for he taught them as one having authority and not as the scribes* (Mark 1:22).

Jesus taught in parables to help people imagine radical ways of relating to God and to one another. Parables such as the Good Samaritan (Luke 10:25-37), Prodigal Son and his brother, his Prodigal Father (Luke 15:11-32), the Lost Sheep (Luke 15:3-7) taught people about the expanse of God's mercy. Jesus used 'similitudes' to explain the mysterious power of the reign of God. The reign of God is *like*: a sower and a seed (Matthew 13:1-9), weeds among wheat (Matthew 13:24-30), a treasure hidden in a field (Matthew 13:44).

Jesus strongly denounced greed. He warned his listeners against the insidious seduction of greed to erode people's wellbeing and communities, *And he said to them, 'Take care! Be on your guard against all kinds of greed; for one's life does not consist in the abundance of possessions* (Luke 12:15). People were drawn to the magnetism of his charism and the power of his message. Jesus proposed a new way of living in caring relationships, relationships that went beyond tribal and filial boundaries (Mark 3:31-34). Jesus ignored certain taboos about touching lepers, relating to women, working on the Sabbath and purity codes (see Mark 3:2). Disciples gathered and followed him with an inner group, symbolised by the Twelve, signifying the new Twelve Tribes of Israel.

Eventually, his teachings so challenged religious authorities that they conspired with Roman authorities to have him put to death, crucified on Calvary. The teachings of Jesus threatened the whole hierarchy of established social and religious order. The crucifixion was the ultimate test of fidelity by Jesus to his passion for God's love for all people. His death was not about reconciling an exiled humanity with God after the sin (*sic*) of Adam and Eve but a terrible price to be paid for utter fidelity to the inauguration of a new time of justice and inclusion. His resurrection symbolised the hope of a transformed life which energised his followers to go forth and courageously preach the Good News.

The creedal statements in the Mass, the *Apostles Creed* or *Nicene Creed* are not especially helpful in proclaiming beliefs about Jesus as the Christ. The creeds are historical documents and move directly from his birth to his death. The creeds omit his teachings about inclusion, reconciliation, prayer, community, justice and relationships with the Father. Discipleship, as a Way of Life, does not even merit a mention in the *Nicene* and *Apostles Creed*. Such basic omissions raise questions about the relevance of the Creeds in the Mass as a faith creedal proclamation by the Eucharistic community. If a Creed is intended as a statement of Christian beliefs and the *Nicene* and *Apostles Creed* ignore the teachings of Jesus, why do we continue to recite them in the Eucharist?

WORSHIP OF JESUS

Throughout the 2000 years of Christian theology and devotions, Jesus as the Christ has been worshipped in an excess of rituals and Christologies (beliefs about Jesus as the Christ). John's Gospel announces the coming of Jesus as the Word made flesh, *And the Word became flesh and lived among us and we have seen his glory, the glory of the Father's only son, full of grace and truth* (1:14). One may understand this advent of Jesus the Word (*logos*) as the coming of Wisdom (*sophia*). Jesus is the manifestation of Wisdom to show us the way to God. In conversation with the woman at the well (John 4) Jesus spoke about his mission, *My food is to do the will of him who sent me and to complete his work* (verse 34).

Billions of Christians throughout the ages have related to Jesus as Saviour, Friend, Lover, Redeemer, Judge, King, Suffering Servant, Merciful God. The oldest known icon of Jesus (3rd century) portrays Jesus as the Good Shepherd. Jesus did not say to his followers 'worship me' but he did say *follow me* (Matthew 4:19).

First century Jews were not so concerned about beliefs but more focused on living moral lives. A person's relationship to God was the foundation of Jewish liturgy. Hence within this Jewish tradition, early Christian doctrinal statements about Jesus did not really assume prominence until after the third century with the emergence of conflicting beliefs and eventually heresies.

The New Testament writers of the Gospels, Acts and Epistles interpreted the Jesus as the Christ within their own Jewish framework of the various feasts, especially Yom Kippur where the High Priest ritualised atonement for the sins of the people. The death of Jesus was interpreted as a sacrificial act to atone for the sins of humankind. Instead of the blood of the slain lamb in sacrifice, now the blood of Jesus on the cross flowed to wash away people's sins (Hebrews chapter 8).

After the fifth century, the doctrine of original sin became an endorsed belief within the corpus of church doctrines. The doctrine of original sin taught that, because of the first sin (*sic*) of Adam and Eve, everyone inherits a residue of sin. During the early Middle Ages, the theory of Atonement was formulated by Anselm of Canterbury (1098) to explain how only someone such as Jesus who was both God and man, could atone for the sins of humankind who had offended a divine Being, God (see Johnson, E. A. *Creation and the Cross: The Mercy of God for a Planet in Peril*, chapter 1).

The so called 'satisfaction' theory of salvation was the answer to Anselm's great question in his book *Cur Deus Homo* (*Why God Became Human*). The doctrine of atonement confirmed the Fall/Redemption Christology and became official church teachings after the Middle Ages.

In today's world, we find it repulsive to be asked to believe that the God of love would require God's Son to die an agonising death as a restoration act for humankind to regain friendship with God. God does not need placating. In atonement theology, creation became separated and marginalised from redemption. After the Middle Ages, creation was increasingly consigned in theology to a mere backdrop to the central drama of individual redemption.

CONTEMPORARY CHRISTOLOGIES

In recent years, there has been a revival of early Christologies as well as a growing movement to situate the Christ story more firmly within the astonishing story of the universe.

There are at least five significant Christologies in contemporary Christian living today.

The first Christology to consider is a focus on Jesus and the reign of God.

A revival of 'reign of God theology' returns us to the dynamic message of Jesus in the Gospels. During my doctoral studies at the University of Notre Dame (USA) in 1970-1972, I recall my excitement when the reign of God insight illuminated my relationship with Jesus – and to think that only happened when I was over thirty years old! Until then, my understanding of the 'Kingdom of Heaven' belonged to what awaited me after death.

The reign of God highlighted the startling teaching of Jesus about inclusion of all, including social and religious outsiders to God's embrace. In a dramatic response to the question of John the Baptist's disciples about his identity, Jesus replied, *Go and tell John what you hear and see: the blind receive their sight, the lame walk, the lepers are cleansed, the deaf hear, the dead are raised, and the poor have good news brought to them* (Matthew 11:4-5).

According to Luke, Jesus began his ministry echoing the stirring call from Isaiah for freedom in God's vision for humanity (Luke 4:18-19). Jesus as liberator sought to set people free of all that bound them into social, religious and physical slavery. With the announcing of the reign of God, a new Exodus had dawned (Exodus 14). His command to those who stood around the tomb of Lazarus is a call for all followers of Jesus, *Unbind him, and let him go* (John 11:44).

The gospel is to set us free! The one criterion for being an authentic reign of God person is a fidelity to doing works of justice (Matthew 25:35-36). Jesus went bravely to his death as an absolute commitment to empower outsiders becoming insiders of God's mercy. The reign of God, the Dream of Jesus is the Dream of every follower of Jesus.

The second theme in contemporary Christology is situating the mission of Jesus with the early Eastern Christian tradition of theosis.

According to the Second Epistle of Peter, we... *may become participants of the divine nature* (1:4). Early Eastern Christianity highlighted how we are made in the image and likeness of God (Genesis 1:27). *Theosis* theology explored how our destiny is to become participants in godliness (deification). The Christology of *theosis* reflected how the mission of Jesus may be appreciated as leading us more fully into the implications of this profound truth of deification, that is, becoming participants in the divine nature of God. Fidelity to the life and teachings of Jesus allows the 'image and likeness of God' to germinate within us. This 'image' is the godliness within us, the divine indwelling. 'Likeness' is the potential movement towards a deepening of the 'godliness', *If you abide in me, and my words abide in you, ask for whatever you wish, and it will be done for you* (John 15:7).

Early Church Fathers such as Irenaeus (130-202) and Gregory of Nyssa (335-395) taught that *theosis* reflected the ideal of a slow spiritual maturation towards union with God. Gregory of Nazianzus (329-390) expressed this wondrous belief, 'Let us seek to be like Christ because Christ also became like us; to become gods through him since he himself, through us, became a man. He took the worst upon himself to make us the gift of the best'. Following the example of Jesus, the 'image' and 'likeness' becomes fused into a oneness with the Source of love. 'Let me show you', says Jesus as the Christ, 'how you may become participants of the divine nature, not as another god, but as a human infused with a divine Presence' (see Romans 8:16-18).

Western Christianity is slowly beginning to embrace the *theosis* Christology of Eastern Christianity which is much more positive about humanity than the Fall/Redemption theology of Western Christianity.

Personally, I am greatly drawn to *theosis* spirituality which is so affirmative of our humanity.

The third theme in contemporary Christology is to relate to a Jesus as the Cosmic Christ or Universal Christ

Jesus as the Christ does not simply belong to a once happening two thousand years ago, but a manifestation of the Divine Energy as the Cosmic or Universal Christ within the whole of creation emanating from the Big Bang or Flaring Forth 13.7 billion years ago. Christ belongs to all people and everything in creation, not just to the Christian community. When Christians imprison Christ within their church, then the Cosmic or Universal Christ departs. St Paul speaks about ...*the glory of Christ, who is the image of God* (2 Corinthians 4:4).

The Jesuit priest, mystic and scientist Teilhard de Chardin (1881-1955) wrote how the Cosmic Christ envisions a universal communion between all men and women in creation, 'All the communions of a life-time are one communion. All the communions of all men (and women) now living are one communion. All the communions of all men (and women), present, past and future, are one communion (*Divine Milieu*, London. William Collins & Sons, 1964, 124). Different religions have different images and icons to express how there is one Great Spirit for everyone and everything in the universe. In 2 Corinthians, we read, *From now on, therefore, we regard no one from a human point of view; even though we once knew Christ from a human point of view, we know him no longer in that way. So if anyone is in Christ, there is a new creation: everything old has passed away; see everything has become new!* (2 Corinthians 5:16-17).

A fourth theme in contemporary Christology is to see Jesus as the Christ within the Wisdom tradition (Sophia, a feminine figure)

In our age of global technology and threats of 'fake news', how does Jesus the Christ as Sophia help us navigate ways to God that are discerned as authentic and wholesome? Jewish Christians associated the *logos* of John's gospel (John 1:1) with Sophia, the feminine Wisdom Woman of the Jewish Scriptures (see Proverbs 8:30-31). For a Christian, Jesus is the light of Wisdom, *Again Jesus spoke to them saying, 'I am the light of the world. Whoever follows me will never walk in darkness but will have the light of life* (John 8:12). How is Jesus the Wisdom Teacher our guide to experience the God of love? Jesus/Sophia is a highly relevant Christology for our cyber era. How do we avoid being seduced by all kinds of siren commercial voices inviting us to dysfunctional lifestyles and choices that contradict the common good? Is discernment an integral feature of our spirituality? A Zen master's advice is helpful about taking time for 'wiping the mirror' so that we can see what really is and not what are afraid to see or what we think we see.

A fifth theme is to relate to Jesus as a Person for us, a very human person

Jesus is not an imperial Judge, King or Lord. He was a Jewish lad who grew up in a tiny remote village of Nazareth, worked probably as a tradesman in the nearby, recently discovered city of Sepphoris. He was profoundly spiritual as a mystic, passionate about justice, both accepted and rejected in his teachings and ultimately paid the ultimate price for his fidelity to inclusion of social outsiders. His suffering on the cross is an act of solidarity with all those who suffer from domestic violence, starvation, social deprivation, wars and mental illness. Raised up by God in resurrection, Jesus as the Christ is a symbol of hope for humanity. Through intimacy with Abba, Father, Jesus is the face of God, *Whoever has seen me has seen the Father... Believe me that I am in the Father and the Father is in me* (John 14:9, 11). This relationship with Jesus gives Christians confidence to face the paradoxes of life. He became one of us. During his brief public teaching, sometimes he was affirmed, on other occasions even his hometown rejected him (Mark 6:1-6). For a Christian, to become more fully human is to become more like Jesus, *From now on, let no one make trouble for me; for I carry the marks of Jesus branded on my body* (Galatians 6:17).

Which Christology most appeals to you now?

INCARNATION

Christians believe that Jesus as the Christ reflected the fusion of humanity and divinity. The Incarnation expresses the faith mystery of 'God in humanity' and 'humanity in God'. Such a belief is not some attempt to reconcile an impossible theological intellectual dualism but reverencing the mystery of Jesus as the Christ as *oneness* in God and humanity. Jesus as the Face of God taught us a way of a relational life that was energised and driven by the power of love, *As the Father has loved me, so I have loved you; abide in my love* (John 15: 9). His mystical experiences with God as Abba impelled him to share this intimacy and show what this intimacy means in daily life. Paul's words echo what discipleship means, *and it is no longer I who live, but it is Christ who lives in me* (Galatians 2:20).

As explained earlier in Room Two, one of the exciting theological developments in Christology is expanding the meaning of Incarnation to situate the advent of Jesus within the first incarnation 13.7 billion years ago through the Big Bang or Flaring Forth (see O'Murchu, D. *Incarnation: A New Evolutionary Threshold* and O'Leary,

D. *An Astonishing Secret: The Love Story of Creation and the Wonder of You*). Such an expanded perspective on Incarnation posits how the incarnation of Jesus as the Christ was not a one-off event that happened two thousand years ago. Christian belief in the incarnation of Jesus is now recovering the cosmic context of the human person Jesus as the Cosmic or Universal Christ (see Rohr, R. *The Universal Christ*) within the evolutionary unfolding of humanity within the universe.

A Remembrance

At the Last Supper, Jesus asked his followers, *This is my body which is given for you. Do this in remembrance of me* (Luke 22:19). How is this 'remembrance' honoured by Christians now, not just in Eucharist, but in a remembering fidelity to his life, teachings and his humanity/ divinity? Christianity is living a way of discipleship not a reciting a series of doctrines about Jesus as the Christ, *For I am convinced that neither death, nor life, nor angels, nor rulers, nor things present, nor things to come, nor powers nor height, nor depth, nor anything else in creation, will be able to separate us from the love of God in Christ Jesus our Lord* (Romans 8:38).

The Eucharist has a cosmic character. The bread and wine, symbols of life and every day eating and drinking, are transformed through faith into the life-force energy of the Body and Blood of Christ, bringing together every element and phase of creation, including us into a communion of love with our Creator God (see O'Loughlin, F. *New Wineskins, chapter 5: Do This in Memory of Me*).

As we open the door to Room Five, we encounter Jesus as the Christ, a friend of our fragile humanity.

Come to me, all you that are weary and are carrying heavy burdens, and I will give you rest. Take my yoke upon you, and learn from me; for I am gentle and humble of heart, and you will find rest for your souls (Matthew 11:28-29).

PERSONAL RESPONSES

GROUP CONVERSATION STARTERS

If you wish to discuss your views of the room with a friend:

1. *What question would you ask of the author if he were present?*
2. *What question aroused your interest in the text?*
3. *What question was provoked by uncertainty or disagreement with part of the text?*
4. *What question arose with a sense of delight or agreement with what you read?*
5. *What further questions have arisen through reading the text of this room?*

DOOR TO ROOM 6
THE CHURCH

Let us open the door of Room Six and enter the room of the Church

How is your membership of the Church significant or not significant in your faith life now?

THE BEGINNINGS OF THE CHURCH

Jesus did not establish a church but he did teach about a way of life. During his ministry, a group of disciples, enthralled by his dynamic teaching and healing, followed him to form the first faith communities. After his death and resurrection the disciples were empowered by the Holy Spirit and began to preach the Good News (Acts 2). And so the church was born. The word 'church' comes from the Greek *ekklesia* meant 'an assembly of equal citizens' which in Roman times was a meeting place. In the early days of Christianity, the followers of Jesus met and prayed together, sharing a Eucharistic meal and serving the poor. At Antioch, the followers of Jesus became known as 'Christians'.

The church is not some kind of enclosed self-sufficient monastery but an intentional faith community whose mission is to celebrate and proclaim the mission of God's revelation in Jesus to foster 'life in abundance' for people and creation. The church has no meaning for itself alone except as a faith community committed to transform the world and the whole of creation through love in God's image and likeness. A Christian community is intended as a visible face presence of a compassionate God in Jesus to the whole world. A dualism which separates church and 'world' makes no sense if Christians take seriously the Incarnation.

The Jesus movement began to spread quickly through the Roman Empire and beyond. An early crisis concerning the status of Gentiles in relationships to Jewish followers of Jesus was settled as a compromise at the Council of Jerusalem 49 CE. It was agreed that Gentile followers of Jesus did not have to become disciples through the way of the Torah. Within a very short time small Christian communities were emerging throughout the Roman Empire and beyond. A turning point in the history of the church was the ascent of the Emperor Constantine in 312 CE who allowed religious freedom for Christians. In 380 CE, the Emperor Theodosius (379-395) declared that Christianity was the official religion of the Roman Empire.

The declaration certainly promoted a rapid dispersion of Christianity to the far reaches of the Empire and beyond. The downside of this proclamation was that it enshrined a political monarchy model of church as the norm for how the church functioned. A hierarchal model of church was reinforced by the work of Pseudo-Dionysius (fifth century) with his description of two hierarchies, a celestial hierarchy and an ecclesial hierarchy.

Because Roman law excluded women's participation in public office, a patriarchal culture became embedded into church culture. Christian theology and structures began to be written within the framework of Greek philosophy, especially the works of Plato and Aristotle. Roman legal framework was the model for church governance. In our modern era, outdated notions of gender discrimination and monarchical authority are simply no longer acceptable in democratically conditioned cultures.

Although the Greek-speaking church had developed the 'sacrament of orders' in the first three centuries (bishops, presbyters and deacons), the clerical state only began to emerge in the fourth century with the fusion of the church governance with the Roman Imperial State.

The recovery of the primal traditions of discipleship in early Christianity is slowly beginning to reappear in this new 21st century era of church life. This recovery retrieves the earliest traditions of how, through baptism, all the faithful have received the *sensus fidei* that is, a sense of God's revelation in Jesus and the Spirit.

A CREEDAL CHURCH OR A REIGN OF GOD CHURCH OR BOTH?

Almost from the beginning of the church narrative, there emerged a basic question which revolved around the tensions between preserving the dynamism of the spirituality of Jesus' teachings about God's mercy, the reign of God and the development of creedal beliefs. Even by the second half of the first century CE, there were different beliefs about Jesus as the Christ.

Confusion arose in early faith communities about what is a 'heresy' and what beliefs in Jesus are faithful to God's revelation in Jesus. Does the church continue to proclaim the spiritual vision of Jesus or does it emphasise historical conditioned beliefs about Jesus? Does assent to Creeds becomes the defining characteristic of being a faithful Christian or does fidelity to the core values of Jesus mark an authentic disciple of Jesus as the Christ?

The words of the Czech Republic theologian Tomas Halik (b. 1948) are pertinent to this tension of seeking to identify teachings that are in accord with the gospel. In an interview with Natalia O'Hara, Halik spoke about the relationship between doubt and faith in our own faith journeys, 'Doubt isn't the enemy of faith but her sister. Unchecked doubt leads to militant secularism but unchecked faith leads to religious fundamentalism'. (*Reform*, November 2010) Seekers befriend doubt as opening new doors to the divine mystery.

It is difficult to overestimate the influence of those early years 312- 600 CE in the Christian story of how the church as institution emerged. The foundational elements of institutional church formed in these years of the Roman Empire persist to this day. Patriarchy, monarchical in character, growing centralisation in authority, top-downward with laity at the bottom of the church pyramid still characterise church governance.

The first sentence in the Introduction from the *General Instruction of the Roman Missal* states, 'The celebration of the Mass is the action of Christ and the people of God hierarchically assembled'. Bishops are accountable upwards to higher sources of authority but never accountable downwards to the laity in faith communities. All these features of church as institution await enduring and serious reform to transform the culture of a centralised monarchical church to one that is more attuned to the spirit of discipleship in Christ.

During the last forty years, there has been a significant collapse of confidence in the institutional Church, especially in the West. How this breakdown of confidence can be reversed will demand radical, imaginative thinking and pastoral planning by the whole People of God. Are church leaders willing and competent in facilitating cultural change for renewal? How might transparency and accountability be embedded into how the institutional church functions? The era of qualified theologians acting out of deference to higher overseeing censoring is over. Is church leadership comfortable and willing with asking the hard questions about the urgency for review of church teachings (see Crothers 90-92)?

How attentively do faith communities respond to the prophetic voices? Is the response of church authority one of discernment, marginalisation or even expulsion? Excluding prophetic voices guarantees death by a thousand cuts from sterile leadership.

Pope Francis is strongly promoting an ecclesiology of 'synodality'. Synodality does not mean organising more synods where bishops meet or dioceses gather for conferences. Synodality is first of all a commitment to an inclusive church, a discernment of the Spirit, conversations, openness to change, research, dialogue and commitment to renewal. The governance structures of a synodal church are modified to authenticate such beliefs within faith communities.

Currently, certain canon laws contradict any notion of a synodal church. For example in the recently concluded Synod on Youth (2018), no lay people could vote. Although the advent of the Plenary Council (2020-2021) in Australia promises significant church reform through commendable wide consultation, current canon law specifications for a Plenary Council reflect a clerical ecclesiology rather than a synodal ecclesiology. Of particular relevance to the Plenary Council are canon laws that state that 'laity may be invited' (canon 443) to participate but have no defining vote and it is the Council of Bishops who set the agenda and questions to be treated (canon 441.4).

How to reconcile the theological dissonance between a clerical orientated ecclesiology through canon law specifications and a synodal orientated ecclesiology will be a challenge for those directing the process to transform church culture. A synodal church does not imply a democracy where everyone has an equal vote but a culture that recognises and affirms the baptismal right of every member to participate in the mission of the church. A synodal church is inclusive and insists as 'a basic justice' that laity become involved in decision making for church life. What features of synodal church governance will look like in practice will need to be addressed as a matter of urgency for church reform to be initiated. (See intending review into management of Australian dioceses and parishes by newly constituted Implementation Advisory Group , May 2019.)

What expectations do you have for the evolution of a synodal church in the near future?

Within the Catholic Church, there are very serious divisions with neo-traditionalist groups, with their own parishes and seminaries, pushing back strongly against the implementation of Vatican II and the leadership of Pope Francis. Such groups harken back to a so-called 'Golden Age' of Catholicism, an illusion because there was never an epoch of Catholicism (or in other Christian churches) without turmoil and struggle (see Chittister, 206). All mainline Christian traditions experience similar tensions between those who resist any changes and those who promote renewal in accord with modern consciousness and fidelity to the revelation of God in Jesus who became the Christ (see e.g. Keith Suter, *The Future of the Uniting Church* Online Opinion Piece).

To balance the negativity of the public face of the church in the media, it is important to recognise that the church as People of God communities flourish and enrich the lives of millions. A proliferation of pastoral services, especially in education, care for the disadvantaged and health care, give witness to the compassionate culture of faith communities. Again and again, throughout over forty years of travels in several countries, I have been in awe of the commitment and dedication of pastors and laity for the less fortunate. When working in the Philippines I deeply admired Catholic justice organisations working to oppose the excesses of the Marcos regime. Religious congregations and lay movements globally strongly promote spirituality and justice in social communities.

Gradually, the epicentre of Christianity is shifting from Europe to other parts of the globe such as in Africa. Although the process of enculturation is slow, at least it is happening to modify liturgy and church teachings away from a European mode and more attuned to diverse cultures. Western European theological and philosophical foundations will gradually be more influenced by indigenous and traditional African, Indian, Chinese, Melanesian religious cultures, cultures which have much to offer Christianity. Even in Western countries, migration has transformed the more traditional Anglo-Saxon-Celtic character of churches to significant multi-cultural and multi-ethnic congregations. Maronite, Syro-Malabar, Chaldean, Ukrainian faith communities are examples of the growing cultural diversity of the previous Anglo-Saxon-Celtic churches.

CRISIS IN CHURCH UNITY

Tragically, the basic unity of the church was fractured by schism (1054) and the Protestant revolt (1517). Currently, there are 38,000 different churches of the Christian faith. During the last century, there have been many ecumenical movements which have impelled most Christian churches to cooperate for the common good and the wellbeing of planetary health.

The ancient Greek word *katholikos* meaning 'according to the whole' began to be adopted (e.g. Ignatius of Antioch 107 CE) to signify 'a within energy to bring wholeness to all' rather than drawing a line for who is inside and who is outside various faith communities. Sadly, the notion of *katholikos* gradually lost its original meaning and historically descended into sectarian divisions between various Christian churches such as 'Catholic' against 'Protestant'.

During the 21st century, there are encouraging signs that this *katholikos* vision of an inner spiritual unifying energy might possibly eventuate. Ecumenical gatherings are much more frequently held now. St Paul reminds all Christians that, underpinning the diversities of various Christian traditions, there is a foundational oneness in Christ, *The bread that we break, is it not a sharing in the body of Christ? Because there is one bread, we who are many are one body, for we all partake of the one bread* (1 Corinthians 10:16-17).

Declining Church Affiliation In Western Christianity

In Western countries, there is a gradual decline of affiliation in church membership prompting urgent calls for renewal of church life. The decline is now reaching a crisis point in most Western countries with less than 10% of mainline Christian church members in regular liturgical participation. A 2016 church survey showed that in Australia, 43% of Catholics who regularly attend Mass were born overseas. The rapid increment of 'nones' (spiritual but not affiliated to religion) in Western countries invites churches to implement new imaginative and even radical approaches in their mission of evangelisation. Christianity in Africa and Asia is slowly moving towards enculturation although the initial 'colonial' foundational heritage still shapes ministry, liturgy and governance in those continents.

The public image of the church has suffered grievously in recent times from revelations of sexual abuse perpetrated by clergy and Religious. It will probably take years for the church as a public expression of God's love and mercy to be restored. An anti-Christian tone in much of the public media does not help in this recovery.

What Is The Future Of Parish For Faith Communities?

A core question is what kind of Christian community is best suited for Christians today? A significant number of Christians today belong to some version or model of localised Base Christian Communities (BCC) rather than parishes. In an increasingly urbanised world are there different models of Christian community which would better reflect how Christians may share and live the Good News? Perhaps smaller, more intimate local clusters of Christian groups may be the way forward for future faith communities. Such a development would necessitate a radical recovery of the first traditions of localised leadership for Eucharistic celebrations (see Moloney, 35-40).

The social fragmentation of Western societies is calling out for the bonding of caring communities. A vibrant parish culture and small sharing groups can address this desire for connectedness. A growing concern in Western societies is isolation and loneliness, especially in the cities. In January 2019, the UK appointed a Minister for Loneliness. Faith communities of their very nature should be gatherings to witness what relationships mean in practical living. Does parish outreach facilitate connections especially those in fragmented/blended families and those living in isolation? Are not the young crying out for friendship/supportive groups? Parishes have a real potential to foster various dimensions of social cohesion between diverse social, multi-cultural and religious groups.

Currently, parish life is greatly enriched by creative and shared leadership where the diverse gifts of the Spirit are celebrated and shared (1 Corinthians 13). Certainly the enduring dead hand of clericalism has no place in the evangelising mission of the church. A vital Christian community, centred on the Eucharist, sacramental life, charismatic renewal, celebration of the liturgical seasons, devotions and caring services offers spiritual and practical support, not just to its members but to the wider community. The mystical/spiritual/justice-orientated church will always exist in tension with the institutional church. Which face of the church will be in ascendency now? How might the mystical face of the church be nurtured through its vibrant devotional, sacramental and contemplative celebrations?

What aspects of mystical spirituality in church traditions attract you now?

From the very beginning of the Christian communities, the celebration of the Lord's Supper or Eucharist has been a central feature of these faith communities (see Luke 22:19; Luke 24:30; 1 Corinthians 11:23; Mark 14:17-31). This centrality of the Eucharist in the traditions of the church raises urgent pastoral questions now about the very nature of priesthood, when millions of Christians throughout the world have no access to regular Eucharist because of a purported 'shortage of priests *(sic)*'. The inaccessibility of people to Eucharist is a consequence of the inflexibility of church governance to modify criteria for Eucharistic leadership, such as mandatory celibacy and gender, rather than a consequence of lack of 'prayers for vocations'. As an option, why not consider a return to the practice of early Christian communities where the designated leader to the community was the leader of the Lord's Supper? (see Schillebeeckx, E. *Ministry: A Case for Change*, 50-52).

The very nature of the church is missionary (see Pope Francis' *Praedicate Evangelium* 'Preach the Gospel', 29 June 2019). The Christian community is on mission to reveal God's love and mercy to all peoples, not only for its own members. The mission of the church is to actively promote 'life in abundance' for everybody and the whole earth community. All its governance, structures, hierarchy, canon law, liturgy, sacramental celebrations, services for the disadvantaged are always 'for' something bigger than itself.

The 'for' is the Spirit energy to bring together humanity and creation into a Oneness with God in love and justice. When church structures and governance no longer serve the Good News, then they must be respectfully modified accordingly. Doctrines are articulated seeking to explain something of the mystery of God's revelation. Beliefs, doctrines and canon laws that do not lead to outcomes for promoting justice and 'abundance of life' have to be critically re-evaluated for their authenticity in the light of the core mission of Jesus. The mission of the church is to be where people are, not locked away in a tabernacle. According to Pope Francis, the church will be like a field hospital, 'bruised, hurting and dirty because it has been out on the streets, rather than a church which is unhealthy from being confined and from clinging to its own security' (*Evangelii Gaudium*, 49).

Christianity in the West seems to have lost much of its energy. How and when revitalisation will happen will require radical and courageous leadership to allow the Spirit to flourish. Pope Francis keeps insisting that the distinct spheres between laity and clergy must be softened. A contemporary ecclesiology will have as its foundation our shared baptism. This baptismal ecclesiology impels *all* Christians to become missionary disciples,

> *For just as the body is one and has many members, and all the members of the body, though many, are one body, so it is with Christ. For in the one Spirit we were all baptised into one body – Jews or Greeks, slaves or free – and we were all made to drink of one Spirit (1 Corinthians 12:12-13).*

To open the door and enter Room Six of the church is to celebrate membership in the Body of Christ.

PERSONAL RESPONSES

GROUP CONVERSATION STARTERS

If you wish to discuss your views of the room with a friend:

1. *What question would you ask of the author if he were present?*

2. *What question aroused your interest in the text?*

3. *What question was provoked by uncertainty or disagreement with part of the text?*

4. *What question arose with a sense of delight or agreement with what you read?*

5. *What further questions have arisen through reading the text of this room?*

DOOR TO ROOM 7
MINISTRY

Let us open the door of Room Seven and enter the room of Ministry
*What is the role of ministry in faith communities? What does ministry
mean to you?*

UNDERSTANDING MINISTRY

One of the most important questions for a faith community is how
the community understands ministry and how ministry is exercised
among its people. By 'ministry' we mean a publicly endorsed activity
by a person in the Christian community who exercises a charism of
the Spirit to promote the Good News of God's revelation in Jesus as
the Christ.

The origins of the word 'ministry' lie in the Greek word *diakonia*
or 'menial service'. The spirit of ministry is poignantly illustrated by
Jesus washing the feet of the disciples at the Last Supper (John 13:1-
20). Ministry is a service not a function or state of entitlement.

Ministry as described in the New Testament, especially in Acts
and the Epistles, situates ministry within five major evangelising roles
of the church:

Diakonia: service to the community especially to the poor;

Kerygma: proclamation or teaching the Good News of the
gospel;

Koinonia: celebration of the community of disciples;

Leitourgia: the worship of the community;

Marturia: witness to the Christian faith.

Rather than speak about 'the mission of the church', perhaps it is more meaningful to speak about 'the church as serving and promoting the mission of Jesus as the Christ'. Ministry is a service to enhance the mission of Jesus as the Christ.

EVOLUTION OF MINISTRY

During the first few centuries of the life of the church, there were several ministries such as waiting at tables, teaching, healing, almsgiving, prophecy, speaking in tongues, discernment of spirits, preaching (1 Corinthians 12:4-11; Romans 12:4-8; 1 Peter 5:1-4). What was emphasised in early Christianity was that ministry was not an expression of authority for its own sake but an act of service for the Christian community.

Fulltime ministries developed as Christianity spread. After 100 CE, the ministries of *diakonos* (deacon), *presbyter* and *episkopos* (bishop) were clearly established in many churches. Great store was placed in the Apostolic Tradition and the significance of the Twelve who were witnesses to Jesus and especially chosen by him. Jesus as Jew was inaugurating a new Israel with the symbolic Twelve Tribes. Likewise is the symbolism of the Seventy (Luke 10: 1-20) who were commissioned by Jesus to go out and preach the Good News.

When the church became more embedded in the juridical and social mores of the Roman Empire, the structure and focus of ministries became more structured. The persecutions and heresies impelled the church to tighten its organisation of ministries with power more consolidated into a top-downward model. The gap between 'clergy' (meaning 'chosen by lot') and 'laity' widened until it became a chasm within five centuries. For the first thousand years, the Christian communities chose their bishops. After 900 CE, the Pope began to influence the appointment of bishops.

During the third and fourth centuries, there was a gradual progression towards the sacerdotalisation of ministry, that is, ministry became more identified with a cultic status. The Jewish hierarchy of high priest, priest and Levite began to be proposed as a desired model for Christian ministry even though Jesus had rejected such a position in his teachings on discipleship.

After the ninth century, altar rails were built to symbolise the differentiation between clergy and laity. During the 12th century, it became official church teaching that through ordination there was an ontological change in the priest, that is, his nature was transformed ('once a priest, always a priest'). This doctrinal movement, so contrary to an understanding of early Christian ministry of Eucharistic leadership, opened the door for a culture of clericalism to flourish.

At this time, the rule of celibacy was enforced, driven by a complex series of forces such as land inheritance, monastic modelling of priesthood, negativity towards sex and exaltation of a celibate way of life as superior to the married state. A review of the whole theology of priesthood might well begin with the formation of priests in seminaries. The current model of separation endorses the seeds of clericalism and entitlement rather than partnership with laity in a shared ministry of service.

The Protestant Reformation (1517) challenged the special mediation role of clergy in the medieval church which taught that the clergy were *the* conduit of God's grace to people.

Although women were very significant in the Jesus story, they were gradually excluded from governance and public ministry. The next room will look more closely at this issue.

CONTEMPORARY CONCERNS ABOUT MINISTRY

At this time in the history of the church with a crisis in ministry, shortage of priests, exclusion of woman, erosion of trust in the clergy as moral leaders, there is a growing movement – especially among Western Christians – to examine the whole theology and practice of ministry, especially ordained ministry. Questions are increasingly asked about such issues as the requirement of celibacy, married priests, clericalism, exclusion of women from ordination and formation of ministers.

A note of caution is warranted when exploring these questions. Any discernment about the ministry of ordination, while eschewing clericalism, should be conducted in a spirit of appreciation for the pastoral dedication of priests.

The constant cry of 'shortage of priests' in Western Christianity is an indictment, not on 'lack of vocations' to the priesthood, but a failure of church leadership to recover a flexible tradition of ministry as exhibited in the New Testament. Jesus did not institute the current canon law specifications for priesthood. Every Christian community has an absolute right to the Eucharist. A few years ago, during a Mass celebrated by an Anglican woman priest, I felt a great sadness to realise that in my lifetime I will never experience a Eucharist celebrated by a woman priest in my own Catholic community.

Formation for those in ministry will include a contemporary appreciation of being actively involved in the church as the Body of Christ, a Spirit-driven service to utilise one's birth gifts for a better world. In the current climate of clergy scandals and critiques of church governance, dedicated pastors of faith communities need affirmation and encouragement to work collaboratively with the laity.

What is your main concern for ministry now?

The gradual movement towards a restoration of the traditions of ministries in the early church is one of the very positive features of modern Christianity. A vibrant parish endorses a whole array of ministries, such as those associated with the liturgical celebrations, RCIA for catechumens, faith education, biblical groups, services to the sick and community needs, sacramental preparations, evangelisation and mission. Do faith communities now need new ministries for emerging social and spiritual needs, such a ministry for loneliness?

> *For just as the body is one and has many members, and all the members of the body, though many, are one body, so it is with Christ* (1 Corinthians 12:12).

As you open the door to enter the Room Seven of Ministry, we might consider what ministries best serve the Good News and how we may participate in ministries.

PERSONAL RESPONSES

GROUP CONVERSATION STARTERS

If you wish to discuss your views of the room with a friend:

1. *What question would you ask of the author if he were present?*
2. *What question aroused your interest in the text?*
3. *What question was provoked by uncertainty or disagreement with part of the text?*
4. *What question arose with a sense of delight or agreement with what you read?*
5. *What further questions have arisen through reading the text of this room?*

DOOR TO ROOM 8 WOMEN AND FAITH COMMUNITIES

Let us open the door of Room Eight and enter the room of Women and Faith Communities.

How do you see the contribution of women in the life of faith communities?

CULTURAL ISSUES ABOUT THE ROLE AND STATUS OF WOMEN

Questions about the role and status of women in faith communities are situated within a much broader context of women in society generally. Patriarchy is deeply embedded in the cultural and social mores of most countries. Ingrained misogyny is so rife that the inferior status of women is simply assumed. In Sri Lanka, for example, a United Nations Report showed that 90% of women are molested when using public transport (*La Croix Internationale*, 6 March 2019). Women are regularly discriminated against in legal frameworks globally.

One in four countries in the world has no legislation to protect women from violent domestic situations. Genital mutilation is still widely practised. Marriage arrangements are biased towards the male and disparity in pay and social status are the norm in virtually all countries. Domestic violence against women is shockingly prevalent. In Australia, on average, one woman a week is murdered by her current or former partner.

It is a serious responsibility of everyone to work towards gender equity and inclusion in every dimension of human activity and social mores.

The emergence of the #MeToo movement is one recent manifestation of protest against sexual oppression and exploitation of women. A very controversial question about women's rights is the relationships between religion and the status of women. According to the Thompson Reuters Foundation survey, the five most dangerous places for women in the world are India, Afghanistan, Syria, Somalia and Saudi Arabia. A disturbing correlation between religion and women's rights is highlighted by surveys that show religion is important is 89% of the population in these countries.

In general, the religions of the world will need to make dramatic and radical changes to abandon misogyny in their governance, theology and anthropology. Currently, the score card for the degree of correlation between religion and women's rights is dismal. According to a New World Health survey in 2017, although Australia is regarded as one of the safer countries in the world for women, it is also one of the least religious. There is no evidence to suggest that religion is a safeguard for women's rights.

Patriarchy And Women In Church Life

The growing impulse in faith communities towards the full inclusion of women is much more expansive than simply a demand for the ordination of women. The impulse is driven by a commitment towards the eradication of an entrenched culture of patriarchy in church life and governance. The full inclusion of women in the life of the church does not begin with women's ordination but with a profound *conversion* of people in faith communities towards deep gender inclusion and equity. Do faith communities facilitate a fusion of the feminine/masculine within their communal cultural character?

Changes to gender inclusion in governance will not bear fruit unless external manifestations of inclusion are founded on an inclusive anthropology and rejection of paternalistic relationships. Members of the faith community will be assisted to foster a holistic appreciation of sexuality. Institutional changes to dismantle patriarchy will always struggle to be implemented if the church culture is mired in the sterile soil of sexism. The dismantling of gender bias must also remove the church teachings against homosexuality as 'inherently disordered'. A Christian anthropology insists for the full inclusion of LGBTQI people into society and church life generally.

To be fair to the Christian churches, faith communities in some countries, especially in Africa and Asia, do engage in commercial and social enterprises that affirm the dignity of women and protect their rights. World Vision International, Caritas, Salvation Army, Voices of Faith, CEDECOL (Colombia), FEDICE Ecuador are a random choice of organisations sponsored by Christian churches which are involved in affirming the status of women in society, refuge houses and promoting commercial enterprises.

Women played a crucial role in the ministry of Jesus. The Gospels record a radical approach by Jesus to women (John 4:4-42; Luke 10:38-42). Faithful to the end, women stayed with the dying Jesus, *Meanwhile, standing near the cross of Jesus were his mother, and his mother's sister, Mary the wife of Clopas and Mary Magdalene* (John 19:25). Mary, the mother of Jesus, was bequeathed by Jesus on the cross as mother of the first community of disciples (John 19:26-27). Women were the first bearers of the news of the resurrection (Luke 24:11; Matthew 28:7). Mary Magdalene was an eminent follower of Jesus and regarded as 'apostle to the apostles' in the early church.

Paul explicitly names women as leaders of early Christian communities. Phoebe is a deacon (Romans 16:1). Maria is a hard worker for Christ (Romans 16:6). Prisca and her husband are co-workers (Romans 16:3). Junia is called outstanding among the apostles (Romans 16:7). Women deacons were active in the early church until at least the fifth century (see Zagano, P. *Women in Ministry: Emerging Questions about the Diaconate*).

The comment of Jesus about the woman who anointed him in Bethany might well be a clarion call for all Christians about the role and status of women, *Truly I tell you, wherever this good news is proclaimed in the whole world, what she has done will be told in remembrance of her* (Matthew 26:13).

The story of faith communities gives witness to outstanding women leaders and spiritual sages. Our own mothers are a good starting point. My mother's deep faith in difficult farming days leaves an abiding influence on my own faith journey. When we reflect on the lives of women such as Dorothy Day, Hildegarde of Bingen, Elizabeth Fry, Joan of Arc, Mary MacKillop, Edith Stein, Rosa Parks, Simone Weil, Teresa of Avila, Jarena Lee, Catherine Booth, Caroline Chisholm, Nasrin Sotoudeh, Founders of Religious Congregations, we recognise how faith communities and society have been enriched by their lives.

> *Which women have inspired you in the past and inspire you now? How would the full incorporation of women in the church change the culture of the church?*

There is a growing, global, social and cultural movement towards gender equality. The roots of patriarchy go back long before the rise of religions in the Axial period. There are diverse and conflicting theories about the emergence of patriarchy as a consequence of the agricultural revolution. Although early images of divine forces were sometimes female, such as the Great Mother, Artemis and Astarte (fertility goddess), more recent religions imaged God as male, implying that the masculine was a superior species.

The philosophies of Plato and Aristotle were significant influences in early Christian thinking. Aristotle held that women were genetically inferior to the male species. Thomas Aquinas followed Aristotle's anthropology and St Paul's words have often been quoted to support misogyny (1 Corinthians 11:10; 1 Corinthians 11:3; Ephesians 5:22). In his great *Summa*, Aquinas held that women were, by their nature, intellectually inferior to men. Aquinas' theology was a dominant theology in the church for eight hundred years. Patriarchy became so embedded into church culture that it will require a momentous and prophetic undertaking to transform this malaise. Church membership, especially its leadership, suffers grievously through the exclusion of women from its decision making and impoverished governance generally.

A demeaning strand in Christian theology linked women with sin and inferiority. Gratian's *Decretum* (1140 CE) which was the first systematic codification of church law stated:

> *The natural order for mankind is that women should serve men... therefore woman is not made in God's image.*

There has been a dramatic shift in cultural consciousness about the status of women during the last one hundred years, especially in Western countries. The political leadership of women and studies in the genetics of sexuality have brought the whole question of women's inclusion to a full participation in church life, including all levels of ministry. Mary, the mother of Jesus, has been a towering icon of an idealised woman and object of devotion since the fourth century. The rising demands for gender equity have left some churches more and more isolated through their designated exclusion of women in leadership and ministry. The self-inflicted wound of patriarchy will not be healed by an outdated appeal to past misogynist practices.

Statements by the church leaders against the ordination of women are not helpful. Some of the reasons previously offered against ordination of women almost belie belief. For centuries, the argument was stated that a priest is *in figura Christi* or *in persona Christi* ('in the image of Christ'). According to this reasoning, because Christ was male therefore a woman could not be priest – as if every priest had to be an Aramaic-speaking, circumcised Jew! Also, such argument seemed to suggest that a woman could not be 'another Christ' – what an insult to every woman!

The rationale against ordination was expressed by Pope John Paul II in the Apostolic Letter *Ordinatio Sacerdotalis, On Reserving Priestly Ordination to Men Alone*, 22 May 1994. He taught that there was an indissoluble link between ordination and the choice by Christ of men only as Apostles. Such a rationale for this teaching would find little support among New Testament scholars today. The Pope's appeal to preserving a long tradition of male priesthood makes no sense in the light of evolutionary cultural and religious transitions.

The argument that the church has never ordained women and cannot do so now because of tradition flies in the face of how-long held beliefs (such as the legitimacy of slavery, freedom of religion) were eventually discarded. To officially declare how God, the creator of the magnificent universe of billions of stars, has decided that women cannot be ordained is a big ask of the faithful in today's social gender consciousness, especially for a younger generation of women. God is beyond gender and really does not have any gender preferences in liturgical leadership.

A CALL FOR FULL INCORPORATION OF WOMEN INTO ALL LEVELS OF SOCIAL AND CHURCH LIFE

There is a growing call, especially in Western orientated countries, for women to be more fully incorporated into all levels of church life, especially its governance structures, leadership including liturgical leadership. Currently, this call has not borne any significant change in church structures in Catholic, Orthodox and some evangelical churches.

The issue of the full incorporation of women into the Body of Christ calls for a *conversion* of heart, heart and mind into the *wholeness* of gender created in the image and likeness of God, male, female and all facets of gender (Genesis 1:27). Faith communities can never authentically fully reflect the 'image and likeness' of God without the inclusion of the life-bearing gift of women. Church governance that excludes half its membership has less and less credibility for the church as a teacher about justice and equity.

Recent popes, including Pope Francis and other church leaders, have reiterated the complementary principle about the roles of men and women in church and society. The complementary principle holds that according to natural law men and women have different talents that should be utilised for families and society generally. Such a principle is deterministic, socially conditioned and simply ignores how both women and men have all kinds of shared talents in leadership, nurturing, physical prowess, and compassion, irrespective of whether they are women or men. The complementary principle simply does not stand serious scrutiny of inclusive gender. A fundamental principle that should be taught, endorsed and implemented in church life must be one of gender equality.

The principle of inclusion in Christ as expressed by Galatians has a long road ahead for fulfilment in several Christian communities, *There is no longer Jew or Greek, there is no longer slave or free, there is no longer male or female; for all of you are one in Christ Jesus* (Galatians 3:28).

When and how might this dream of Paul be realised now in faith communities?

As you open the door of Room Eight for Women and Faith Communities, consider how a holistic appreciation of gender leads to an inclusive faith community.

PERSONAL RESPONSES

GROUP CONVERSATION STARTERS

If you wish to discuss your views of the room with a friend:

1. *What question would you ask of the author if he were present?*
2. *What question aroused your interest in the text?*
3. *What question was provoked by uncertainty or disagreement with part of the text?*
4. *What question arose with a sense of delight or agreement with what you read?*
5. *What further questions have arisen through reading the text of this room?*

DOOR TO ROOM 9
A CHRISTIAN ETHICAL
WAY OF LIFE

Let us open the door of Room Nine and enter the room of A Christian Ethical Way of Life.

What are key issues in Christian moral teachings today?

MORALITY IN THE PUBLIC DOMAIN

How do Christian moral teachings shape the way I live? How do I live a virtuous life?

Our media is awash with news of wars, terrorist bombings, domestic violence, cyber bullying, torture, wars, entrenched poverty and racial discrimination. Fake news communicates confusion and falsehood. Instagram was the most widely used cyber bullying network in Australia in 2017

Evil acts are a consequence of choices in human behaviour. Moral evil contradicts the very heart of the teachings of Jesus about the 'abundance of life' (John 10:10). Is it a linguistic accident that the word 'evil' is 'live' spelt backwards? Tension between virtue and sin is always ever present on our media screens and daily encounters. Every day people make moral choices about their behaviour. Do I call in work claiming a 'sickie' and then go off with my mates for a game of golf? Do I pay a just wage to a fruit picking iterant worker who cannot speak English?

We might ourselves consider these four questions about our own moral choices:

What ethical codes influence these choices?

How does our Christian faith shape our moral code in day-to-day living?

How does one live a virtuous life?

What is the relationship between an ethical following of Jesus and publically endorsed ethical codes of secular societies?

The most enduring question in the story of religions and morality is what are people's motivations for following a religion's teaching on moral codes? Is the motivation based on fear of eternal punishment such as, 'Do this otherwise you will go to hell!'? Or is the motivation one that is much more benign by wanting to do the right action out of love or natural goodness? Is choosing a moral act driven by a desire for fidelity to God's will? It is only a generation ago that Catholics were told that it was a mortal sin to miss going to Mass on Sunday. Traditionally, moral teachings from the church emanated as a series of 'Divine Commands'.

All religions promote ethical ways of living. In Buddhism, the Noble Eightfold Path; Hinduism the Dharma; in Islam, the Qur'an and sayings of Muhammad; the Torah of Judaism... all describe or teach ethical ways of life. Sometimes, religious morality of one tradition conflicts with the morality of other religious traditions such as the conflicts about religious tolerance between Christianity and Islam in certain countries where apostasy from Islam is punished by the death penalty.

The 13th century Sufi poet Rumi spoke about the universalism of morality:

Out beyond ideas of right and wrong
there's a field.
I'll meet you there.

Recent public disclosures, such as the Royal Commission into Institutional Responses to Child Sexual Abuse (Australia) 2013-2017, which exposed abuse by people in ministry, seriously compromised the integrity of the church as an authentic moral teacher. There is no easy solution to how the church will restore its credibility in the public domain as a respected moral voice in influencing government legislation on such issues as refugees, same-sex marriage, human cloning, assisted dying, palliative care, eugenics and religious freedom.

CHRISTIAN FAITH AND MORALITY

Christian faith is both personal and social. The gospel leads us to union with God as a personal conversion. However, this personal conversion always includes social action for the wellbeing of others and earth care. The Progressive Christian movement has tended in the past to emphasise the evolution of doctrinal beliefs rather than Christianity as a transformative movement in social justice and human dignity.

Jesus taught a way of living not a series of doctrines to be followed. Scripture scholars point out that most of the teachings of Jesus were about having right relations with others. The Epistle of James is especially blunt on this question, *If a brother or sister is naked and lacks daily food, and one of you says to them 'Go in peace keep warm and eat your fill' and yet you do not supply their bodily needs, what is the good of that? So faith by itself, if it has no works, is dead* (James 2:15-17).

As we enter this room of a Christian Ethical Way of Life, we are aware that there is an abundance of resources on every aspect of moral theology and Christian ethics. There is no intention here of attempting any summary of this corpus of teachings on Christian morality, merely to give a *flavour* of some of the themes within contemporary thinking about Christian ethics. In today's world, there so many moral issues that are complex in their diversity such as Voluntary Assisted Dying (VAD), same-sex marriage, refugee migration, equity in wealth distribution, climate change, religious freedom, social media, multiculturalism and social cohesion, harvesting organs, integrity in social institutions (e.g. Royal Commission into Misconduct in the Banking, Superannuation and Financial Services Industry, 14 December 2017 – 4 February 2019).

Sometimes, there is no simple answer to what is morally right or wrong. Certainly, we know that there are historical shifts in thinking about moral stances according to new insights regarding the human condition. For example, advances in genetics and the social sciences are slowly modifying traditional church teaching on LGTBQI people, sexual identity, blended families, divorce and bioethics. The Synod on Young People *The Faith and Vocational Discernment* (2018) showed that for many young people, church teachings on sexual morality were incomprehensible. How the teaching church will modify its teachings and then develop pastoral strategies to communicate these teachings are PRIORITIES for the church to connect with a younger generation.

MAJOR SHIFTS IN CHURCH MORAL TEACHINGS

One of the major shifts in thinking about moral theology has been the movement from the classical way of stating moral conclusions from fixed abstract principles to historical consciousness of the cultural context within which these teachings emerged. For example, we now condemn slavery as a moral evil whereas for most of Christian history slavery was not regarded as such. Other examples of how our moral code has shifted are previous church teachings on usury (charging of interest on money), religious freedom, the death penalty, environment and divorce.

A classical approach to moral teachings insists that there are unchanging universal principles that are time honoured and integral to natural law. An historical approach recognises basic principles of human behaviour but these principles are always open to development as our consciousness is modified in the light of insights from anthropology, psychology and sociology. Our own moral awareness is not a static condition but evolves out of reflections on life experiences. Our conscience is transformed by life encounters such as work with refugees, people with disabilities, visiting those in prison or those who live below the poverty line.

A further element in church teachings illustrates how these teachings may conflict with core values held by society generally. A recent example of this conflict was highlighted in the same-sex marriage debates. The church argued that sexuality between members of the same sex is always intrinsically evil according to natural law. An oppositional approach held strongly by a majority of the population insisted that the church's position violated the natural rights of people. There is also a massive dissonance in traditional church teachings on homosexuality as 'intrinsically disordered' and the growing public awareness that a significant number of the clergy are gay (see *Los Angeles Times Survey* 13 December 2013). The phrase 'intrinsically disordered' is demeaning of gay women and men and urgently needs to be erased from church language and teachings.

A rapidly evolving area of moral teachings is within the ethics of ecological responsibilities. Due care and kinship of environment are not ethical options for Christians but rather basic moral imperatives. In *Laudato si* (2015), Pope Francis is quite explicit on the essential commitment to kinship with creation, 'Living our vocation to be protectors of God's handiwork is essential to a life of virtue; it is not an optional or a secondary aspect of the Christian experience (217)'.

The emergence of the feminist movement is bringing a healthy wholeness to living a virtuous life through an impulse towards gender equality. Christian morality will always lack a definitive integrity unless women are fully involved in its formation and teachings. A Christian anthropology implies a reciprocity of discerned wisdoms between women and men in any exposition of a moral life according to a holistic way of living. To what extent have the voices of women been influential in the formulation of Christian ethics?

There is a delicate balance between holding firm to what is intrinsically good for humankind and creation and what is a capitulation to the latest cultural manifestation of relativism. The modern shift in moral theology is a movement away from a law obligation approach to a much more personal, relational model of being human. In an age of excessive individualism, however, it is all too easy to assume moral positions which arise out of hedonism and disregard of the common good. While the movement towards a relational model tends to discard a 'black or white' approach to morality, the discourse about *situation ethics* (see Fletcher, J. *Situation Ethics: The New Morality.* Westminster. John Knox Press, 1997) illustrates the complexity of making moral decisions.

Situation ethics proposes that moral rulings depend on the life circumstances of the people making such judgments. Critics argued that such a position is a slippery slope with the ever-present danger of leading to moral anarchy because it leaves moral choices to the whim of the individual. The mantra of relativism is, 'If I think it is okay to do this, then it is okay!' Relativism in moral decision making is a consequence of rejecting certain core principles of holistic morality and endorsing individualism as the benchmark for moral decisions.

The Cardijn tradition in making moral decisions proposes a threefold movement of 'See, judge, act', that is, awareness, discernment and then intentional action according to an informed conscience.

A credible teaching church on ethics is enjoined to forge close partnerships with those competent in the area of ethics inclusive of laity (women and men) as well as moral theologians. The encyclical *Humanae Vitae* (1968) on birth control took the final position of just four delegates and discarded the reservations of the opposing fifty-seven delegates. A key factor in making the definitive teaching was a purported continuity with traditional church teachings (*Casti Connubii* 1930).

The widespread disregard of this teaching by a great majority of married Catholics was a watershed in the perception of the church as a credible moral teacher. Negativity about sexuality has been a major historical problem for the veracity of the church's moral teachings and a source of erosion of confidence in church teachings. A teaching church should always be, first, a listening, learning discerning church.

It is critical for faith communities to seek a discerned balance between holding fast to core moral teachings grounded in the Christian Story and yet be receptive to evolutionary shifts of consciousness about the human condition within the context of creation. Moral teachings are formulated through a process of communal listening, discernment, scholarship and a willingness to acknowledge the implications of evolving consciousness in modifying moral teachings. The Christian church can never be some kind of self-contained bubble remote from the rough and tumble of moral dilemmas in society and human behaviour. Its role is to engage with secular agencies to transform the cultural mores towards 'life in abundance', a just society and kinship with creation. Christian living is much more than a series of 'do's' and 'don'ts' but a way of living in a wholesome manner that affirms individual and communal wellbeing.

What is critical for Christians is that faith communities are firmly grounded in basic principles of moral Christian teachings and accountable to an enhancement of holistic living in the wider human and earth communities.

Do faith communities give witness to core principles of Christian morality?

FOUNDATIONAL PRINCIPLES IN CHRISTIAN MORALITY

A series of fundamental principles shapes the character and orientation of a virtuous life according to the Christian faith. Most of these principles would be endorsed by other religious faiths as well as social agencies although the language, beliefs and modes of expression would differ from a Christian articulation of principles.

These principles may be stated as:

People are created in the image and likeness of God and are worthy of dignity and respect (Genesis 1:27).

Christian ethics has the life and teachings of Jesus as foundational elements in its proclamation.

We are created as relational people and choose to live as an interconnected humanity.

Society should respect and protect all human life from conception to death and work towards the common good.

The principle of the common good implies an absolute commitment to justice in creating a participative society where the basic rights of all people are respected. The words of Micah sum up this principle, *and what does the Lord require of you but to do justice, and to love kindness, and to walk humbly with your God* (Micah 6:8).

Humanity lives within the web of life connectedness within the whole of creation. Therefore humans have an ethical responsible to care for their common home of creation itself (*Laudato si*, chapter 4: *Integral Ecology*).

The laws of society should enhance the wellbeing of its citizens and the natural world.

Two basic principles in Christian social teachings are subsidiarity and solidarity. Subsidiarity means that decisions about issues of justice are made as closely as possible to the grass roots as good government allows. Solidarity means that we have a shared responsibility for each other, *If one member suffers, all suffer together with it* (1 Corinthians 12:26).

Every person is entitled to basic human rights as formulated by the *Universal Declaration of Human Rights* proclaimed by the General Assembly of the United Nations, 10 December 1948.

There is a primary right of individual conscience although this right is governed by reason and discerned divine law.

Although there are moral laws in Christian ethics, these laws must support the pastoral care of people.

The Ten Commandments, the Beatitudes and the *Judgment of the Nations* (Matthew 25:31-46) are foundational cornerstones for living an ethical life.

A selection of principles from religious traditions

Seek good and not evil,
That you may live;
And so the Lord, the God of hosts, will be with you.
Amos 5:14.
Treat not others in ways that you yourself would find hurtful.
Buddhism

This is the sum of duty: do not do to others what would cause pain if done to you.
Hinduism

Not one of you truly believes until you wish for others what you wish for yourself.

The Prophet Muhammad, *Hadith*

Do not do unto others whatever is injurious to yourself.

Zoroastrianism

MORALITY AND EVERYDAY LIVING

One of the most significant happenings in Christian ethics and moral teachings is bringing morality into everyday living. A virtuous life is not reserved to making momentous ethical decisions far removed from real life but trying to live a good moral life in day to day circumstances. The moral essence of the Ten Commandments and the Beatitudes is expressed in what our responses to what each day brings in seeking to live as a faithful disciple of Jesus. One cannot really separate a moral life from spirituality. Of its essence, a Christian spiritual life is a commitment to living and nurturing 'life in abundance' (John 10:10).

Which moral issues seem to be the most challenging in our society now?

The cornerstone of Christian ethical living is a faithful response to the core belief that *God is love, and those who abide in love abide in God, and God abides in them* (1 John 4:16). The energising power of love infuses our connectedness with self, others and creation.

FORGIVENESS AND RECONCILIATION

We all make mistakes and commit sin. There were three crosses on Calvary, not one. The harsh reality of sin is poignantly illustrated by Jesus crying out in his death agony surrounded by two thieves (Luke 23:32-34). The sinfulness of the two thieves hangs beside a merciful

God in Jesus. Our own sinfulness is an invitation to turn again to the embrace of God's mercy. Pope Francis spoke about this need for restoration and reconciliation, 'The most important thing in the life of every man and woman is not that they should never fall along the way. The important thing is to get back up, not to stay on the ground licking your wounds' (address to 300 USA bishops in Washington, 23 September 2015).

A feature of church life is the rituals, sacraments and teachings on forgiveness and reconciliation. As sinful people, God's forgiveness is always reaching out in compassion, mercy and love. The parable of the Prodigal Son and Prodigal Father (Luke 15:11-32) images this refrain of mercy. God *reaches out* in compassion. The Prodigal Father *went out* to meet his son. The dying cry of a crucified Jesus echoes the plea for forgiveness, *Then Jesus said, 'Father, forgive them; for they do not know what they are doing* (Luke 23:34). The church must likewise reach out to her people and gather them together in forgiveness rituals such as the sacrament of Reconciliation, the Third Rite of Reconciliation or communal rites of forgiveness.

The ongoing conversion through awareness of our own sinfulness may lead a person to new depths of compassion. A compassionate life (compassion: *cum* 'with', *passio* 'weep') touches into the compassion of God's mercy for those struggling to lead an ethical life, driven by the impulse of love. Our moral fragility is an invitation to seek forgiveness.

> *In everything do to others as you would have them do to you;*
> *for this the law and the prophets* (Mathew 7:12).

As you open the door and enter Room Nine of a Christian Ethical Way of Life, reflect on your own ethical journey.

PERSONAL RESPONSES

GROUP CONVERSATION STARTERS

If you wish to discuss your views of the room with a friend:

1. *What question would you ask of the author if he were present?*
2. *What question aroused your interest in the text?*
3. *What question was provoked by uncertainty or disagreement with part of the text?*
4. *What question arose with a sense of delight or agreement with what you read?*
5. *What further questions have arisen through reading the text of this room?*

DOOR TO ROOM 10 CHRISTIAN SPIRITUALITIES

Let us open the door of Room Ten and enter the room of Christian Spiritualities.

What evolving themes in your spirituality are important to you now?

SPIRITUALITY IS FOR EVERY PERSON

Every Christian is called to live a life of holiness. The very idea of holiness may evoke images of saintly people with halos around their heads instead of a harassed single mother trying to work out where the next meal is coming from to feed the family. A basic belief in Christian spirituality is that everyone is destined to become more fully human in the image and likeness of God (Genesis 1:27).

Spirituality is an enduring motif in the story of humankind. Anthropologists and palaeontologists uncover evidence of art, rituals, burial sites and, more recently, writings that seem to confirm how some form of spirituality is in the very DNA of the human species, especially in *homo sapiens*. So widespread among later species of hominids are their rituals and art that some writers have suggested that the human species may be called *homo religious*, indicating a universalism of spiritual orientations within the human person.

Spirituality is a response to an inner restlessness within our soul, a restlessness that cries out for ultimate meaning. The words of

St Augustine echo this restlessness, 'You have made us for yourself, O Lord, and our hearts are restless until they rest in you' (see Rolheiser, chapter 1). Nevertheless, the growing phenomenon of atheism might well give pause to designating our species as *homo religiosus* and challenge any assumption that spirituality is integral to our DNA.

TWO MAJOR PATHWAYS IN TRADITIONS OF SPIRITUALITY

Throughout history, there have been two major traditional pathways to spirituality. The pathways are *Kataphatic* spirituality and *Apophatic* spirituality.

Kataphatic spirituality (Greek: 'to bring God down to be able to speak about God'). This strand of spirituality is articulated through words, rituals, actions, music, dance, reading, art, worship and icons. *Kataphatic spirituality* is the normal way in which people express their spiritual life by doing things.

Apophatic spirituality (Greek: 'to describe the way of what may not be said about God'). This strand of spirituality is a movement of the listening heart (*shema* : Hebrew) rather than intellectualise or articulate about spirituality. Words and actions seem inadequate to express a relationship with God. *Apophatic spirituality* involves a reflective silence in contemplation which allows God to touch the Inner Self of one's being.

Authentic spirituality is the inner journey from what is called the False Self or Outer Self to the True Self or Inner Self. Religion that functions only in the False Self places great emphasis on simply performing religious duties in a kind of righteous manner. Spirituality that is grounded in True Self is a conversion or *metanoia* (Greek: 'change to a new consciousness') or deep inner encounter with the Divine Presence (see Rohr, R., *Immortal Diamond: The Search for Our True Self,* chapters 1 and 2). Such a conversion is described by Paul in Romans as, *Do not be conformed to this world, but be transformed by the renewing of your minds, so that you may discern what is the will of God – what is good and acceptable and perfect* (Romans 12:2).

Christian spirituality is the lived experience of an unfolding personal journey towards a wholeness (holiness) in union with God through Jesus and the Holy Spirit. The life and teachings of Jesus offer pathways towards this desired union with God. Jesus as prophet and healer teaches us how to experience the tender compassion of God (Luke 10:25-37). The practices of spirituality are woven through the events of everyday and commitment to kindness (see Room One). The spiritual life soon withers unless it is nourished by prayer and meditation.

The Hebrew word associated with the word for prayer *tefillah* ('being connected', 'think', 'blessings') expresses the essence of prayer as 'being connected' with a loving God, inner self, others and creation. At the core of Christian spirituality there resides the faith stance of God's love for each one of us and the energising Spirit throughout creation. Jesus stands as witness to who God is and who we might become. In Philippians, we are urged, *Let the same mind be in you that was in Christ Jesus* (Philippians 2:5).

A vital feature of spirituality is *compassion* (Latin: 'weeping with'). The defining word to appreciate 'compassion' is 'with'. A compassionate way of living is to be *with* someone, not above them in status or education or patronage but a sense of companionship. The concept of 'mercy' may suggest a response to someone in need from a superior / inferior mindset. However, an expression of compassion is not merely a gesture of 'standing with' someone but what follows from being compassionate.

Through references to the actions of the Dalai Lama and Archbishop Desmond Tutu, Garry Everett in his article 'Worse things than Dying' makes the point that 'Compassion is not enough. It is generosity that makes the difference... generosity is about giving of yourself and your time and resources (John Menadue 'Pearls and Irritations' 18 April 2019)'. The largesse of generosity is grounded in discerned action and personal involvement. There is the critical price of personal investment in acts of compassion through displacement from our securities and our vulnerability.

If spirituality is important to us, then we will give time and energy in nurturing its growth. A spiritual life soon withers into indifference unless we take seriously the challenge of being proactive about our faith journeys. Do we set aside time for reflection, reading (*Lectio Divina*), prayer, service works, spiritual guidance, participation in the sacramental life of the church?

SPIRITUALITY FOR EVERYONE

The history of Christian spirituality exhibits how rapidly spirituality became the exclusive reserve of the clergy, monks and Religious with the laity a poor fourth in ranking order of eminence. The *Catholic Encyclopedia* (1914) was quite explicit on this 1000 year old assertion; 'But the laity are not the depositaries of spiritual power; they are the flock confided to the care of the shepherds ...' One must hasten to add, however, that there is an abundance of lay people and lay groups throughout the centuries who were outstanding in spirituality such as Jean Vanier, Martin Luther King, John Wesley, William and Catherine Booth, Elizabeth Fry, Caroline Chisholm, C. S. Lewis, William Wilberforce, Eric Liddell, J.R.R. Tolkien, Rosa Parks, Dorothy Day. The roll call of canonised saints in the church however is heavily weighted on the side of the clergy, monks and religious.

Whereas Protestant Church traditions have generally avoided the clergy/lay dichotomy in teachings and practices of spirituality, the Catholic Church is more recently slowly recovering the early church traditions of discipleship for laity. A shared baptism does not differentiate between archbishop and street sweeper. Multicultural and ethnic influences shape the orientation of spiritualities and devotions. A revival of Celtic spirituality is a reminder of the vast treasure house of traditional spiritualities.

What are some spiritual practices that you would recommend?

Spirituality has become popular in the public domain and can mean anything from tai'chi, bush therapy, wakei-seijyaku, crystals, devotions in a church, music, icons, caring for the homeless and mindfulness. Christian spirituality aspires to union with God and service to others and creation. Practising Christian spirituality may involve a wide spectrum of devotions and practices such as prayer, meditation, sacraments, pilgrimages, Eucharist, Bible and services to the poor, all leading to being at a oneness with God, self, others and creation.

Everyone is so different and will engage in the spiritual journey in ways that are unique to that person. To live ways of being spiritual is to intentionally invite the faith presence of the Spirit to be woven into every facet of our daily lives. That I can walk or stand, speak or hear, laugh or cry – all doings and emotions evoke a profound sense of gratitude for the blessings of just being alive. According to Meister Eckhart (c1260 – 1329) 'If the only prayer I ever said was a prayer of thanksgiving that would be enough'. Why does the Eucharist (Greek: *eukharistia* 'thanksgiving') begin with 'Let us call to mind our sins'? Why not, 'Let us call to mind in thanksgiving the many blessings of our life' and then say, 'Let us call to mind our sins'?

In today's world, a spiritual life struggles against the headwinds of a culture saturated with materialism, atheism and indifference.

A spirituality that does not flow into a passion for justice has little if anything to do with Christian spirituality. According to the Last Judgment scene (Matthew 25:34-41), there is one and only one criterion of being a faithful follower of Jesus, *for I was hungry... I was thirsty... I was a stranger... I was naked... I was in prison... just as you did it to the least of these who are members of my family, you did it to me.* Religious talk about spirituality that is not expressed in action for 'life in abundance' is nothing more than hot air. Since, through baptism, Christians become members of the Body of Christ (1 Corinthians 12:27), then they continue the 'abundance' mission of Jesus to bring God's gracious presence to the world (see Rolheiser 75-76).

A MODEL FOR SPIRITUAL JOURNEYS

The motif of the journey is a popular image for the unfolding story with its ebbs and flows of a person's experience of spirituality. The Emmaus story (Luke 24:13-35) images an archetypal narrative of how people encounter the hidden Christ on their faith journeys.

A model for the spirituality journey might be described as a three stage movement:

Kenosis or emptying or 'letting' go (Philippians 2:6-8) of the demands of False Self, narcissism, pride, focus on exteriors of life, devotions without interiority.

Communion by seeking connections and relationships with others and creation, we grow in compassion and kindness.

Oneness or the union with God and all things is a descent to the True Self (see Stockton, E. *Martha and Mary of My Mind: Studies in Deep Consciousness,* 32-33).

The theologian Karl Rahner SJ (1904 - 1984) suggested that the future Christian would be a mystic or nothing at all. Decades ago, he wrote, 'The devout Christian of the future will either be a "mystic", one who has "experienced" something, or cease to be anything at all'. The eminent scientist Albert Einstein (1879-1955) once said, 'If we are not mystics, we might as well be dead'. Mystics go beyond externals and appearances. They are not people who live in cloudland but people who are drawn to the very core of their spiritual centre, the True Self to encounter God there.

According to the medieval mystic Meister Eckhart, 'My work is to free myself of myself so that You can be born in me'. St Symeon the so-called New Theologian (10th century), wrote, 'The greatest misfortune that can befall you as a Christian is not to know consciously that God lives within you'. Mary's response of *let it be* (Luke 1:38) to the angel's invitation is a model for all Christians to allow the Holy Spirit to give birth to Christ within us. Mystics have been saying for centuries what modern science, especially quantum physics, is telling us now about the interconnectedness of all energy fields, a scientific dictum that aligns with a religious belief about the energy of *oneness* with God.

The quest for union with God in Christ and the Spirit is a humbling and joyous experience. Being involved in regular meditation will lead us into this experience. I might offer reservations about the spiritual journey as a 'joyous experience' with the qualification of how tough sometimes is the quest to lead a spiritual life.

One of my experiences in Israel is almost a parable of this struggle. I arrived by bus at the foot of Mount Tabor, the traditional mountain of the transfiguration (Luke 9:28-36). Rather than take the bus up the winding road to the top of the mountain, I decided to push my way through the tangled undergrowth towards the top of the mountain. It was arduous going, made more perilous by an Israeli military helicopter suddenly hovering above me with a soldier, riding shotgun and eyeing me carefully in binoculars. Deciding I was simply a harmless stupid tourist, the helicopter peeled away. When I reached the mountain top, my arms rather scratched but exalting at the 360 degree view, I recall feeling energised, transfigured. A spiritual journey to transfiguration involves lots of scratches and struggles against the thick undergrowth of our human frailty.

Each of us might wish to choose our own spiritual mantra that is like our spiritual compass pointing to true north of our spiritual pathways.

A spiritual mantra that attracts me is:

> *From now on,*
> *let no one make trouble for me:*
> *for I carry the marks of Jesus*
> *branded on my body* (Galatians 6:17).

As we open the door and enter Room Ten of Christian Spirituality, let us allow the Spirit to experience a ONENESS with God and creation.

PERSONAL RESPONSES

GROUP CONVERSATION STARTERS

If you wish to discuss your views of the room with a friend:

1. *What question would you ask of the author if he were present?*
2. *What question aroused your interest in the text?*
3. *What question was provoked by uncertainty or disagreement with part of the text?*
4. *What question arose with a sense of delight or agreement with what you read?*
5. *What further questions have arisen through reading the text of this room?*

DOOR TO ROOM 11
FAITH COMMUNITIES IN
A GLOBAL WORLD

Let us open the door of Room Eleven and enter the room of Faith Communities in a Global World.

How do you see the role of a Christian in the world today?

CHRISTIANITY FOR THE WHOLE WORLD

The global world of communications, commerce and international travel involves us in the world, at least in a marginal way. Breaking News in a 24/7 media cycle alerts us to the latest catastrophes in local and far-away places.

How does a Christian respond to a global awareness or is one merely content to live out one's Christian faith in a localised community? Do you ever feel almost emotionally overwhelmed by the endless succession of media reports on violence, floods, fires, car smashes, shootings, bombings, robberies and weeping survivors?

The world's population is expected to reach eight billion people by 2030. About one quarter of the world's population live on or below the poverty line. In 2018, 600 million lived in extreme starvation. Currently, there are increasing movements of people from areas of economic deprivation, religious and political oppression as well as threats to environmental consequences from climate changes. As a balance to this pessimism, it should be noted that, overall, the world's population living standards have risen in terms of general health and economic wellbeing. The downside of this rise in global wellbeing is the massive disparity of wealth distribution and incremental destruction to the biosphere.

RELIGIONS AND THE WORLD

The majority of the world's population is significantly influenced by the religious traditions of Hinduism, Christianity, Islam, Buddhism and Judaism. Indigenous peoples struggle to retain their original cultures in the face of intrusive globalisation. World-wide technology exerts a powerful influence on the cultural mores of countries as do international corporations on world economies. The percentage of Christians in the world remains fairly steady at about 32%.

What role does Christianity have today in the world order and the natural world? How does the mission of God in Jesus as the Christ transform the world and creation towards 'life in abundance'? The church is not an entity for itself but an intentional faith community committed to celebrate God's love in Jesus and enhance the lives of all peoples and creation. Can Christian faith communities make a difference in promoting justice and peace in the world? They certainly can't do this without an attentive listening and cooperative action with secular societies and other religious traditions. A retreat into purported securities of traditional theological certainties simply builds walls against any prospect of being an effective transformer of culture for justice and earth care.

Throughout its 2000 year old history, a dominant strand of traditional Christianity diminished the significance of ordinary life happenings and focused on issues more associated with redemption and salvation. The Second Vatican Council was quite explicit on the role of the church in the world. According to *Gaudium et Spes*, 'The church, inspired by no earthly ambition, seeks but a solitary goal: to carry forward the work of Christ himself under the lead of the befriending Spirit' (no. 3). The 'work of Christ himself' embraces the whole earth community.

> *What could faith communities do more to promote a more just society?*

During the 21st century, there is a growing movement towards an eco-centric context for reframing traditional Christian theologies and spiritualities. While each faith tradition will seek to clarify and share its own corpus of beliefs and spirituality, the mission of the church surely is to be fully integrated into a global vision and shared commitment to the entire earth community (see Preston, N. *Ethics: With or Without God,* 49). There is no long term future in identity religions that posit exclusive and bigoted ideologies. On 7 January 2019, Pope Francis spoke to 180 ambassadors in Rome about the urgency to resist the growing nationalistic movements across the globe and return to multi-nationalism for the common good. The 13th century Persian poet Rumi's verse offered wise advice against religious sectarianism:

> *The religion of love is apart from all religions.*
> *The lovers of God have no religion but God alone.*

The Christ story has faced many challenges during its 2000 year old faith journey. From a tiny frightened group of disciples, faith communities have spread to every corner of the globe with about two billion Christians. The Judaeo-Christian influence has been a major force on Western culture and, indeed, world culture. Throughout the world, Christian communities now provide an extensive array of services especially in education, health care, environment, welfare, arts and community justice projects. The church as a reconciler and hospitality harmoniser has an urgent role for the faith communities today to combat racism, tribalism and populism.

According to Sr Patty Fawkner SGS, in her article *Stranger-guest-host relationship*, '... something is happening throughout the world that is threatening the intrinsic human nexus between stranger, guest and host. At times with strident dog-whistling and race-baiting, at other times more dangerously subtle, we recognise a deliberate calibrated injection of fear. Fear of the one who is different, who doesn't look like me, or believe like me' (*The Good Oil* November 2018). Terrorism emanating from the extremes of white ethnic nationalism and Islamic jihadism generates division rather than harmony in societies.

The fragmentation of communities and polarisation into identity blocs contradict everything that Christianity should uphold. Authoritarian regimes are springing up all across the globe. Faith communities have the potential to reconnect God, humanity and the cosmos into a communal harmony (see, 'Cosmotheandric' principle of Raimon Panikkar, Room Two). How is the church implementing its charism of reconciliation?

What are some of the biggest threats to religion in the world today?

Sadly, the church has sometimes been a force for regression of people's basic rights. Recent exposures of the shadow side of church culture, such as in the finding of the Royal Commission into Institutional Responses to Child Sexual Abuse (Australia 2016-2018) have diminished the credibility of the church as a moral teacher. Numerous instances of child sexual abuse by clergy and Religious in several countries have created a major crisis for church leadership and loss of morale in church communities.

GLOBAL CHALLENGES TO CHRISTIANITY

The decline of Christianity in Western orientated cultures has been hastened by a whole series of factors such as the power of dominant materialism, international multi-corporations, a choice culture, rigidity of churches to modify governance, doctrines, and gender discrimination. In the face of growing aggressive secularism, the church has often been on the defensive in public discourse about contraception, same-sex marriage, voluntary assisted dying and homosexuality. A growing disconnect between the official teaching church and its members, at least in Western countries, has widened with little evidence of a significant reversal of this trend (see Allen, J. L. *The Future Church: Trend One: A World Church* 13-53).

One response to the churches to modernity and calls for renewal has been to revert to an evangelical fundamentalism and pull down the shutters against unwanted intrusions to perceived venerable truths. Another response from 'seekers' is to effect more discerned radical changes in their churches. Such changes will take many years to become embedded in church culture.

The Catholic Church made a bold leap for reform in the Second Vatican Council 1962-1965. The reform movement faltered under Pope John Paul II and Pope Benedict XVI. Pope Francis has energised the Catholic Church to return to the dynamic power of the gospel although he is facing fierce opposition from conservative forces. Progressive Christian movements in Protestant churches, especially in USA are striving to celebrate the Christian Story within the context of modern consciousness and studies. Other major church traditions such as Orthodox, Lutheran, Uniting, Methodist, Pentecostal, Baptist and Anglican pursue their own renewal according to their own traditions. The growth of Christianity in Africa and Asia has accentuated the movement away from a European styled Christianity.

Contemporary studies on the New Testament and the Christian story have generated a whole series of challenging questions about historical accretions in governance, ethics and doctrines which impede the dynamism of the Good News. There will always be a degree of tension between the institutional church and its mystical/spiritual heritage. The dominance of the institutional/doctrinal church in previous centuries has marginalised the mystical strands in the Body of Christ. There are encouraging signs in contemporary church life that the mystical/spiritual aspects are now emerging in a new spring-time of spirituality.

As people become more educated with ready access to information on the internet, there is an increment in questions from 'seekers' concerning church teachings and worship. Does church life today faithfully reflect God's revelation in Jesus as the Christ? Are there historical accretions in the Christian story that need to be consigned to the libraries of history so as to allow an evolutionary progression of God's revelation in Jesus to emerge through Spirit discernment? Such a commitment will demand prophetic and courageous leadership for this to happen. The warning of Jesus about the futility of applying old practices of church life to new challenges is pertinent for today's church, *No one sews a piece of unshrunk cloth on an old cloak, for the patch pulls away from the cloak, and a worse tear is made. Neither is new wine put into old wineskins; otherwise, the skins burst, and the wine is spilled, and the skins are destroyed; but new wine is put into fresh wine-skins, and so both are preserved* (Matthew 9: 16-17).

As discussed in Room Two, modern science, especially quantum physics, cosmology, evolution and ecology, have changed many of the philosophical foundations of traditional Christian theology. In the light of a creative partnership between religion and science, Christians are encouraged to communicate their beliefs in language and metaphors that are in accord with the wisdoms of modern science and modern consciousness. A commitment of faith does not imply that Christians leave their intellect at the church door. To persist in proclaiming the Good News in a pre-modern consciousness is to reinforce alienation, not only from a younger generation, but many thinking educated Christians and certainly from 'seekers'.

In some countries, especially China, North Korea, India and the more extreme Islamic countries, persecution of Christians is widely prevalent and legally constricted in the public domain. In thirty-six Muslim-majority countries, religious freedom is not permitted or severely confined. The church's own history of opposition to religious freedom, especially from the fifteenth to the early twentieth century, is itself an indictment on its historical maxim that 'error has no rights!' It's only in the previous one hundred years that religious freedom has been officially enshrined in church teachings (see e.g. Vatican II document *Dignitatis Humanae* 7 December 1965). The church has a prophetic role in promoting religious freedom throughout the world by drawing out lessons from its own dismal record of religious oppression. (See Philpott, D., 'A pathway to freedom', *The Tablet*, 30 March 2019.)

Opposition to the Christian Story is more subtle in Western countries. The malaise of materialism seeps into the very fabric of society and dulls the heart's openness to spiritual perspectives on life. In the Statistics Netherlands (CBS) Report, 50% of its people now indicate that they are not religiously affiliated. Does Christianity have a viable future in the West?

CHRISTIANITY AS A MAJOR FORCE FOR GOOD IN THE WORLD

To portray faith communities as communities in crisis only would distort the enormous positive contribution of Christianity to world culture, its major services, especially in education, welfare and health care, and especially spiritual sustenance to billions of people. After all, through the resurrection of Jesus and a positive anthropology, Christianity is a religion of hope. Such a hope is not some kind of fanciful illusion but a faith belief in God's love for each one of us within this bounteous world.

There are so many examples of vitality in faith communities, such as World Christian Meditation, strong assertive actions for social justice, affirmation of ecological projects, lay spiritual groups, outstanding witnesses to the gospel, peace mediators by bishops and pastors in countries riven by tribal strife. World movements such as the World Charter for Nature (ratified by the United Nations 1982) and the Earth Charter (launched 2000) are examples of global initiatives that demand support from faith communities.

How can faith communities do more to enhance the wellbeing of the biosphere? Currently 20% of the world's population use 80% of its resources. With the population moving towards nine billion people by the end of the century, this situation simply can't continue, especially with climate change and global warming.

What can be done to assist people who have to walk for an hour to get a bucket of drinkable water and wash their clothes in the river far away from where they live? What are we to do about the situation in the polluted Mediterranean Sea where a whale was found with 28 kg of plastic in its stomach? Such a disturbing prognosis calls the world's people to a profound change in the ways we live and consume. How might faith communities assist in this shift of consciousness? What, realistically, can countries do to respond to the flood of people seeking a better life in migration?

During the 21st century, a great enterprise for Christianity will be to pursue a *deep ecumenism* (see Hans Kung and the Global Ethic Foundation) whereby the notion of a global communal ethic shared for all humanity will be promoted and communicated (see Preston 34-35). The concept of *deep ecumenism* does not suggest various religions renouncing their own ethical teachings but in fostering partnerships for shared ethics that support the dignity of all people and creation. A major impulse now in Christianity is the beginning of a movement to reframe the Christ story within the story of the universe. Deep ecumenism embraces every member of the earth community, not simply those in religious affiliations.

There are many encouraging signs that the Spirit is calling faith communities to a third great era of transformation: from its foundations within a Jewish religious culture to the second dominant era of Roman and European framework; and now to the third significant emergence era where God's revelation in Jesus and the Spirit is celebrated and lived within the story of the universe. There is an understandable reluctance from some church leadership to let go some historical accumulations in the Christian story that no longer resonate with an evolutionary consciousness. Cultural and institutional change generates anxiety and resistance. However, the Christian Story is too precious to be entombed in a museum of relics rather than a Spirit-energised Body of Christ.

Of its very nature, the church is missionary. The core impulse of a faith community is to proclaim and celebrate the Good News. In this era of a crisis, at least in Western Christianity, the faith community must not lose confidence in its mission and fall back into a defensive and apologetic mode. The DNA of the faith community is evangelisation. The final injunction of the resurrected Christ to his disciples was, *Go therefore and make disciples of all nations, baptising them in the name of the Father and of the Son and of the Holy Spirit, and teaching them to obey everything that I have commanded you* (Matthew 28:19). Mark's Gospel states this proclamation in an even broader vision than Matthew's. According to Mark, *Go into the world and proclaim the good news to the whole creation* (Mark 14:15).

A new era for Christianity is already with us. Are Christians ready to respond to the challenges for evangelisation? Let the New Story for Christianity be told and celebrated!

See, I am making all things new (Revelation 21:5)

PERSONAL RESPONSES

GROUP CONVERSATION STARTERS

If you wish to discuss your views of the room with a friend:

1. *What question would you ask of the author if he were present?*
2. *What question aroused your interest in the text?*
3. *What question was provoked by uncertainty or disagreement with part of the text?*
4. *What question arose with a sense of delight or agreement with what you read?*
5. *What further questions have arisen through reading the text of this room?*

Open the door to Room Twelve and what will you experience?

POSTSCRIPT

KNOCK ON THE DOOR OF DIVINE INVITATIONS
AND JOYOUSLY ENTER A ROOM OF DIVINE LOVE

Gracious God,
Help me to open doors
To enter the room of my deeper self
To bring love and kindness to others
To enhance and live within the
wellbeing of the earth community.

May I dwell in this room of oneness with you.

Amen.

Resources

Allen, J. L. Jr. *The Future Church: How Ten Trends are Revolutionizing the Catholic Church*. New York. Doubleday, 2009.

Armstrong, K. *A History of God*. London, Vintage Books, 1999.

Armstrong, K. *Fields of Blood: Religion and the History of Violence*. London. The Bodley Head, 2014.

Apostolic Exhortation of the Holy Father Francis *Gaudete et Exsultate (On the Call to Holiness in Today's World)*. Strathfield, NSW. St Pauls Publications, 2018.

Bessler, J. A. *A Scandalous Jesus: How the Three Historic Quests Changed Theology for the Better*. Salem, Oregon. Polebridge Press, 2013.

Cannato, J. *Radical Amazement: Contemplative Lessons From Black Holes, Supernovas, and Other Wonders of the Universe*. Notre Dame, Indiana. Sorin Books, 2006.

Cannato, J. *Field of Compassion: How the New Cosmology Is Transforming Spiritual Life*. Notre Dame, Indiana. Sorin Books, 2010.

Chittister, J. *The Way We Were: A Story of Conversion and Renewal*. Maryknoll, New York. Orbis Books, 2005.

Christian, D. *Origin Story: A Big History of Everything*. UK. Allen Lane an imprint of Penguin Books, 2018.

Crothers, J. *The Clergy Club*. Hindmarsh, SA. ATF Publishing Group, 2018.

Delio, I. *Making All Things New: Catholicity, Cosmology, Consciousness*. Maryknoll, NY. Orbis Books, 2015.

Delio, I. *The Unbearable Wholeness of Being: God, Evolution, and the Power of Love*. Maryknoll, NY. Orbis Books, 2013.

De Waal, F. *Mama's Last Hug: Animal Emotions and What They Teach Us about Ourselves*. UK. Granta, 2019.

Edwards, D. *Ecology at the Heart of Faith*. Maryknoll, New York. Orbis Books, 2006.

Edwards, D. *Partaking of God: Trinity, Evolution, and Ecology*. Collegeville, Minnesota. Liturgical Press, 2014.

Encyclical Letter of Pope Francis *Evangelii Gaudium* (*The Joy of the Gospel*). Strathfield, NSW. St Pauls Publications, 2013.

Encyclical Letter of Pope Francis *Laudato si* (*On Care for Our Common Home*). Strathfield, NSW. St Pauls Publications, 2015.

Fox, M. *Original Blessing: A Primer in Creation Spirituality*. Santa Fe, New Mexico. Bear & Company, 1983.

Fox, M. *Meditations with Meister Eckhart*. Santa Fe, New Mexico. Bear & Company, 1983.

Johnson, E. A. *Ask the Beasts: Darwin and the God of Love*. London. Bloomsbury, 2014.

Johnson, E. A. *Creation and the Cross: The Mercy of God for a Planet in Peril*. Maryknoll, NY, 2018.

Johnson, G. I. *A New Spiritual Tapestry: Woven from the Frayed Threads of Traditional Christianity*. Fire-Light Books, 2018.

Krauss, L. M. *The Greatest Story Ever Told... So Far: Why Are We Here?* London. Simon & Shuster, 2017.

Lao-tzu (translated by Stephen Mitchell). *Tao Te Ching: The Book of the Way.* London. UK Kyle Books, 1996 (Cathie edition).

MacGregor, D. *Blue Sky God: The Evolution of Science and Christianity.* Alresford, Hants.UK. Circle Books, 2012.

Maher, A. (ed.) *Faith and the Political in the Post-Secular Age.* Bayswater, Vic. Coventry Press, 2018.

Mahoney, J. *Christianity in Evolution: An Exploration.* Georgetown, Washington, DC. Georgetown University Press, 2011.

Martin, S. *Cosmic Conversations: Dialogues on the Nature of the Universe and the Search for Reality.* Franklin Lakes, NJ. New Page Books, 2010.

Moloney, F. J. *Broken for You: Jesus Christ: The Catholic Priesthood & The Word of God.* Bayswater, Vic. Coventry Press, 2018.

Mudge, P. *Living Spirituality: A Quadrivial Model of Spirituality for Teachers, Parish Workers & Lecturers* (Series 1). Baulkham Hills, NSW. Snap Printing (privately published), 2019.

Newell, J. P. *The Rebirthing of God: Christianity's Struggle for New Beginnings.* USA. SkyLight Paths Publishing, 2015.

Nolan, A. *Jesus Today: A Spirituality of Radical Freedom.* Maryknoll, NY. Orbis Books, 2007.

Nowotny-Keane, E. *Amazing Encounters: Direct Communication from the Afterlife.* Melbourne, Australia. David Lovell Publishing, 2009.

O'Leary, D. J. *Travelling Light: Your Journey to Wholeness.* Blackrock, Dublin. Columba Press, 2001.

O'Leary, D. J. *The Healing Habit*. Dublin. Columba Press, 2016.

O'Leary, D.J. *An Astonishing Secret: The Love Story of Creation and the Wonder of You*, Mulgrave, Vic. Garratt Publishing, 2018.

O'Loughlin, F. *This Time of the Church*. Mulgrave, Vic. Garratt Publishing, 2012.

O'Loughlin, F. *New Wineskins: Eucharist in Today's Context*. Bayswater, Vic. Coventry Press, 2019.

O'Murchu, D. *God in the Midst of Change: Wisdom for Confusing Times*. Maryknoll, NY. Orbis Books, 2012.

O'Murchu, D. *Incarnation: A New Evolutionary Threshold*. Maryknoll, NY. Orbis Books, 2017.

Parkinson, L. *Made on Earth: How Gospel Writers Created the Christ*. Richmond, Vic. Spectrum. 2015.

Preston, N. *Ethics with or without God: Christianity and Morality in the 21st Century*. Preston, Vic. Mosaic Press, 2014.

Preston, N. *Exploring Eco-Theology, Eco-Spirituality and Eco-Justice*. Workshop address at Common Dreams Conference, Sydney, August 2017.

Rohr, R. *Immortal Diamond: The Search for Our True Self*. San Francisco. Jossey-Bass. A Wiley Imprint, 2013.

Rohr, R. *Just This: Prompts and Practices for Contemplation*. Albuquerque, New Mexico. CAC Publishing, 2018.

Rohr, R *The Universal Christ: How a Forgotten Reality Can Change Everything We See, Hope For and Believe*. London. SPCK, 2019.

Rolheiser, R. *Seeking Spirituality: Guidelines for a Christian Spirituality for the Twenty-First Century*. London. Hodder and Stoughton, 1998.

Sanguin, B. *The Way of the Wind: The Path and Practice of Evolutionary Christian Mysticism.* Vancouver. Viriditas Press, 2015.

Schillebeeckx, E. *Ministry: A Case for Change.* London. SCM Press LTD, 1981.

Stockton, E. *Wonder: A Way to God.* Lawson, NSW. Blue Mountain Education and Research Trust, 2018.

Treston, K. *Who Do You Say I Am? The Christ Story in the Cosmic Context.* Northcote, Vic. Morning Star Publishing, 2016.

Treston, K. *The Wind Blows Where It Chooses: The Quest for a Christian Story in Our Time.* Bayswater, Vic. Coventry Press, 2018.

Toews, J. E. *The Story of Original Sin.* Eugene, Oregon. Pickwick Publications, 2013.

Wohlleben, P. *The Secret Wisdom of Nature: Trees, Animals, and the Extraordinary Balance of All Living Things.* Vancouver/Berkeley. Greystone Books. David Suzuki Institute, 2017.

Wohlleben, P. *The Hidden Life of Trees.* The Illustrated Edition. Trans Jane Billinghurst

Vancouver/Berkeley. Greystone Books. David Suzuki Institute, 2018.

Zagano, P. *Women in Ministry: Emerging Questions about the Diaconate.* Mahwah, New Jersey. Paulist Press, 2012.

GENERAL

The Tablet (International Catholic Weekly)

National Catholic Reporter

WCCM (The World Community for Christian Meditation)

WATAC (Women and the Australian Church)

APCVA *Progressive Christian Voice* (Australia) Inc (APCVA)

Accent Publications (New Zealand) www.accentpublications.co.nz

UCFORUM (Progressive Sources Education Sites)

The Swag: Quarterly magazine of the National Council of Priests of Australia

SOCIAL MEDIA

Richard Rohr: Daily meditations

Jesuit Communications: editor@pray.au

Emmaus Productions and Monica Brown. Thornleigh, NSW (02) 94840252

Discerning Hearts Podcasts

YOUTUBE CLIPS: (NOTE - A SAMPLE ONLY)

Richard Rohr

Wayne Dyer

Thomas Berry and the Earth Community (6 minutes)

Brian Swimme: The New Story (6 minutes)

Ilia Delio: Evolution: a Christian Perspective (Teilhard de Chardin) (8 minutes)

John Haught: God after Darwin (16 minutes)

Joanna Macy: The Great Turning (5 minutes)

Bruce Sanguin: Evolutionary Christianity (7 minutes)

PERSONAL ROOM FOR CHRISTIAN LIVING

After reflecting on the various rooms of Christian living, compose your own ROOM.

According to my Christian faith, I make this statement about my ROOM: